Twayne's English Authors Series

Sylvia E. Bowman, *Editor*

INDIANA UNIVERSITY

Lawrence Durrell

Lawrence Durrell

By JOHN A. WEIGEL

Miami University

Twayne Publishers, Inc.   ::   New York

PR
6007
.U76295
1966

66673

For Sara Ruth Watson

Preface

A book may be defined as an event between a writer who believes he has something to say and a reader who has a reason to listen to that something. This book is addressed to readers who want to know about Lawrence Durrell and his writing. Comprehensive rather than specialized, it does not attempt to top the many competent but briefer studies that have appeared in the United States and abroad. I have tried to survey all the significant items in the extensive and complicated Durrell canon, but I have had to allot my limited space proportionately; consequently, many minor items are not mentioned. My study has, I hope, only one obvious bias: I admire Lawrence Durrell and respect his work.

I am indebted to the goodly host of scholars and critics who have reviewed, analyzed, and evaluated Durrell's work-in-progress. I have read hundreds of pages of sincere and provocative comment in scores of periodicals, but I have not attempted a definitive bibliography, nor can I hope to acknowledge all my indebtedness. The libraries of Harvard University, Yale University, and Miami University have served me well; and several student-friends (a category mixing duty and affection) typed and commented and then typed again. My thanks go to the following: Sue Roberson, Deborah Coffin, Linda Thompson, Kathy Davis, Gordon Friedman, Peter Buirski, Ruth Yeakle, and Joel Baron. And special thanks go to three good friends—Patricia Staebler, Warren Staebler, and Milton White—and to one good editor—Sylvia Bowman.

Lawrence Durrell was informed that this study was being written, and courteously—as always—did not forbid it. He is responsible, of course, only for what *he* wrote and not for what *I* wrote about what he wrote.

Permission to quote from the various works of Durrell published in the United States by E. P. Dutton and Co. has been granted by the publisher.

JOHN A. WEIGEL

Miami University
Oxford, Ohio

Contents

Chronology

1912   Lawrence G. Durrell born on February 27, 1912, in Jullundur, India, of Protestant-Irish-English stock. Childhood is
backdropped by Tibetan mysteries.

1923   Larry in school in England: Tibet gradually becomes only
a memory. Larry, no great scholar, will not attend a university; but he reads and dreams and reads some more.

1933   Lawrence, now of age, begins to live: he plays the piano,
races cars, and hates England. He also reads, talks, and
makes friends.

1935   Durrell publishes his first novel, *Pied Piper of Lovers* (of
which the literary world takes slight notice) and marries
Nancy, an artist. He discovers Henry Miller's *Tropic of
Cancer* and writes to Miller in August of 1935 (from Corfu)
warmly praising *Tropic*. An important friendship begins.
An important year.

1936   The Durrells—including Lawrence's mother, sister, and
two brothers—are now settled in Corfu, swimming and
sunning. A good time begins.

1937   Under pen-name of Charles Norden, Durrell publishes
Panic Spring. The switch in names does little good, but
the book is really his first significant performance. After
this, Durrell's work shows the spark ignited in him by Miller (and by others he is reading and meeting). Durrell is
writing almost-important poetry too.

1938   *The Black Book* is published—in Paris, for it is too naughty
for England and America. (Later it is republished with
profit in both places.) Durrell is finding his own voice now;
T. S. Eliot, for one, hears him. He meets Miller in Paris,
and they validate their letter-writing friendship in person.

1939 Miller visits Durrell in Corfu: the last happy time before war comes.

1940 "Exile" and war-service, first in Greece and then in Egypt: a series of experiences which contribute much to later writings. From the "assignment" in Egypt comes the material for *The Alexandria Quartet*.

1943 Durrell still in Alexandria, but his wife and daughter have gone to Palestine.

1945 Durrell in Rhodes as government official: material for *Reflections on a Marine Venus* just as Corfu has been material for *Prospero's Cell*.

1947 Durrell marries for the second time. His assignment in Argentina is depressing, but he works up lectures on poetry and plans a "reader" of Miller's works.

1949 Assignment in Yugoslavia with Foreign Service furnishes material for thriller-novel (*White Eagles Over Serbia*) and time to work on sketches and poems. Durrell cables Miller to withdraw *Sexus* as bad book, but later Durrell recants and Miller forgives.

1952 Durrell moves to Cyprus, takes job as teacher: material for *Bitter Lemons* and gestation time for the *Quartet*.

1953 Durrell does a "Darley" on Cyprus: teaching, writing, minding the baby.

1956 Revolution in Cyprus ends that island interlude. After Cyprus, Durrell tries Dorset, England. He finishes the book about Cyprus, *Bitter Lemons*, and works on *Justine*.

1957 Durrell moves to a cottage in Provence. He has decided "to live or die by writing." He writes and he lives. *Justine* is published. It is a literary and financial success.

1958 *Balthazar* (written in six weeks) and *Mountolive* (written in twelve weeks) are published in England. The ball (as well as the *Quartet*) is now rolling. "Success" is assured: book clubs, American publications, and invitations to speak.

1959 *Mountolive* book club choice in the United States. The interviewers, reporters, young writers, and fans descend on the cottage in Provence. The simple life is threatened.

1960 *Clea* (written in eight weeks) is published. *Now* the critics begin to condescend, for success is equivocal. Durrell has

been honest. He says: "I try to give value for money."
But how much of a man does one own for the price of a
book?

1961 The marriage of Durrell and Claude, a writer, is reported
in the papers. The theater now beckons. Durrell's play,
Sappho, is performed at the festival in Edinburgh. Critics
praise the play as literature rather than as drama. Durrell's second play, *Acte,* is performed in Hamburg. Durrell,
working with the great Gründgens, is modest, honest, and
eager to learn.

1964 Durrell's third verse play, *An Irish Faustus,* also performed in Hamburg, is followed by ambivalent critical
verdicts. Durrell's career now pauses to gather strength,
possibly for a reach toward greatness.

Lawrence Durrell

CHAPTER 1

Lawrence Durrell: Professional Writer

LAWRENCE DURRELL is both charming and honest. He has
many friends. Although somewhat below average in height,
he is physically strong. He does whatever he does enthusiastically
and often expertly. He swims, builds walls, makes love, describes
places, tells stories, sings songs, plays the piano, and paints pictures. But his *profession* is writing.

Born in 1912, Lawrence Durrell has packed his fifty-odd years
full. When the young Durrell discovered Henry Miller in 1935, he
was ready to put the world in order. Miller "fertilized" him, and
Durrell went to work. In a youthful rhapsody called *The Black
Book* he lashed out against England and the death he smelled
there. He was not posing. He was telling the truth. He hit as hard
as he could because he cared deeply. And T. S. Eliot noticed
him and praised him.

In psychological terms, Miller motivated him, but Eliot reinforced him. Durrell responded with dignity and gratitude. He
succeeded. He had been a respectable but moderately obscure
writer long before *The Alexandria Quartet* brought him fame and
fortune. But with the publication of *Justine* he flashed, and
clever critics also struck pay dirt. *Justine,* they said, was subtle.
It needed explicating. When Durrell began to clear things up
himself—by confounding and elaborating the "plot" in subsequent
volumes—the same critics despaired. They lamented the disappearance of the austere irony of *Justine.* Durrell was losing control, they feared. It is, however, the assumption of this study of
Lawrence Durrell as a writer that he has always been in control
of his material: he writes as he wants to write. Also, it may be
assumed, he lives as he wants to live—within the limits of certain
realities.

Durrell's self-awareness includes the consciousness of a public image which he has taken some casual care to keep focussed. In a letter to Henry Miller in 1958, Durrell wrote of the "perplexity" he was causing his "fans" who couldn't place him either as Wodehouse or as Joyce.[1] Durrell is versatile but he is not confused. He ranges widely and pays the price. He is often contrasted with himself. He may *really* be more of a poet than a novelist, more of a travel-book writer than a dramatist, more of a wall-builder than a painter; but the world is less dull because he has appeared in it.

After the pictures of Durrell big as life appeared in *Life* and his fame was established, some sober American literary critics turned perplexity into hostility. *Success* often embarrasses academic sensibilities. But there's nothing wrong with Durrell's own sensibility. His integrity, tempered with irony, is still intact. It's just not easy to deal critically with a contemporary who persists in commenting, reprinting, and experimenting without regard for sober literary biography which seeks a theme that may hold throughout a lifetime.

Lawrence Durrell, with his abundance of talent and charm and his healthy scorn for foolish consistency and petty botanizing, has enjoyed perplexing others. Thus the various tapes, interviews, studies, and accounts of his life and works tend to be either pompous or trivial; for Durrell is genuinely both exuberant and humble. The universe to which Durrell belongs is a heraldic one, not a rational or logical one.[2] His vision is an artist's, yet he is a professional writer, one who gives his readers value for their money; and he has often called attention to the fact that he writes for a living. He defies categories. One can order the events in his life and indicate the patterns sufficiently to project the man as artist, but in the end one must remain somewhat perplexed— or take refuge in over-simplification.

He can be arch or ironic, but the more one studies Durrell's life and works the surer one becomes that he means what he says —at least *when he says it.* Ironic he must be at times, for irony is the last defense of intelligence against dullness, and irony acknowledges the complexity of truth. Thus Durrell has pleasantly called de Sade a rationalist and himself a dervish, acknowledged Groddeck, Miller, Lawrence, Eliot, Auden, or Dylan Thomas respectively as a major influence—gently condescending to be important enough to have influences. But in general he resists formulas and categories.[3]

By now Durrell as a writer has become a public property. The essential Durrell, however, survives the interviewer, the critic, and the biographer. Although as a professional he accepts the need to be an image, the specifications of that image are less important than the truth of the flash of that image as it is recorded at a given moment.

Durrell, like every man, has a life, and his life, like the life of every man, is both private and public. Real privacy, which is more than a wall around a yard, should not be invaded; for that is scandal. Durrell has been married three times as of this date (1964), and this fact is interesting without further conjecture. His friend, Alfred Perlès, called Durrell the "eternal husband" type.[4] Popular magazines, which like to print quasi-intimate and exclamatory pictures of the private lives of the famous and infamous, have from time to time shown pictures of Durrell and of his friends; and such camera studies, despite their frequent vulgarity, seldom fail to reveal sensitive and perceptive faces.

I *Early Days*

Durrell was born on February 27, 1912, in Jullundur, India, of an Irish mother and an English father. Confounding genes and place, one can give him an interesting heritage. It is likely that Durrell himself, in the letter to Henry Miller in which he described his childhood as "a brief dream of Tibet until I was eleven," was more poet than chronicler. "The horoscopes cannot touch me," he wrote to Miller in 1937. "I'm already mad!" [5] India, Ireland, and England—all left marks on him, but in what proportions it is not easy to say.

As a pre-adolescent he moved to England, where he attended school—many schools, according to his own word; but he never entered a university. The pattern of many-schools-sans-university and the casual experimenting with jobs (from playing the piano in night clubs to automobile racing) is characteristic of the young man of talent and integrity in the 1930's. Durrell's own awareness of the interesting aspects—as well as his objective acceptance of the hardships—of not conforming to the university pattern correlates with his glamorizing the memory of his childhood in India. So it was in character for him, as a young man in the dreary English winter, to propose that the family, at the time consisting of Lawrence, his mother, a sister, and two brothers, all leave England for a more congenial climate. How they moved to Corfu is told charmingly by brother Gerald, now a successful naturalist, in his story of the Durrell family called *My Family and Other Animals*.[6]

Lawrence Durrell at twenty-three, attractive in person, healthy and casual, began his productive professional life with the discovery of Henry Miller—and his personal life with his marriage to Nancy, an artist. The marriage did not survive, and what happened to it is a private matter; but what happened between Miller and Durrell does survive and has literary as well as personal implications, and it is of concern here.

II Miller and Durrell

Henry Miller is a controversial figure, and the best way to deal with him is to insist on controversy just as he himself has. He *risked* starvation in order to create; that he has not starved is irrelevant. A student of Durrell's works must know Miller, and Miller's canon is extensive and complicated. Time was when the major Miller items were not available over the counter, but the recent reprintings of the *Tropics* and other works make it possible now to test firsthand Miller's significance.[7] Occasionally an irate citizen takes steps to prevent young students from reading Miller, but by and large the impact of the Miller protest, its insouciance, its guts and sperm and blood—a protest which excited young Durrell in 1935—has already become a tradition.

It is now a matter of history, not controversy, what happened to the twenty-three-year-old Larry Durrell when he first read *Tropic of Cancer* and, very importantly, had sense enough to write to the author about the book.

The young Durrell had already published one indifferent novel, *The Pied Piper of Lovers*, when in August, 1935, he wrote the letter to Henry Miller that began their friendship. (The following account of the enduring relationship between Durrell and Miller relies heavily on the published correspondence, which is sensitively edited by George Wickes. Page references to the edition listed in the "Notes" to this chapter are given in the text in parentheses after each citation.) In his first letter to Miller, Durrell congratulated the novelist on having "dunged under" all his contemporaries. He regarded *Tropic* as the "copybook" for Durrell's generation, and there could be no more enthusiastic praise (4-5). Miller replied that Durrell's was the first "intelligent letter" about *Tropic* that he had had from a Britisher, and he agreed with Durrell's estimate of the importance of the book. In fact, Miller's excitement about his own work remained an appealing quality in Miller throughout the correspondence.

By the spring of 1936 Durrell apologized for his own "new and facile novel" (*Panic Spring*) which had none of the anguished intensity and integrity of Miller's work. Durrell asked for news from Paris. Miller's replies referred to surrealism, Lao-tse, and Jack Kahane of the Obelisk Press, who was then publishing banned and sensational works. Durrell, although indicating interest in "movements," feared he would never join one, being himself an "ardent Durrealist"(24). By the end of 1936 Durrell announced that he had a contract with Faber and Faber to publish *Panic Spring* (which he disparaged), but his poems (which he liked) had been rejected. He was also now deeply involved with *The Black Book,* which, he shouted, is "good"(33).

Durrell has always taken his poetry seriously, and his references to it in the correspondence with Miller seldom met an appropriate response from Miller; but by the fall of 1936 Durrell had opened his heart to his friend: he confided in Miller his concept of the "heraldic universe" and his excitement about his own poetry. He wanted to destroy time, and in heraldry the creative moment is free from time. In one letter he exclaimed: "I'm writing such poetry these days, such poetry!"(28).

Durrell was twenty-five in 1937, a year packed with significant moments for the young man. Durrell had acknowledged Miller's influence on *The Black Book,* and Miller liked the work tremendously: "Your commercial career is finished," Miller predicted (72). (But Miller was wrong!) At this time Durrell announced that he was "the first writer to be fertilized by H.M."(90). He campaigned for the recognition of Miller's greatness. Durrell, concerned with his own integrity, asked if he should expurgate *The Black Book* for Faber and Faber. "No," Miller emphatically answered. Durrell retorted in capital letters: "I CAN'T WRITE REAL BOOKS ALL THE TIME" (104).

In September, 1937, Miller and Durrell met in Paris. Finding one another compatible in person, they validated the series of confidences they had been exchanging. Their mutual friend Alfred Perlès vividly describes the meeting at the Villa Seurat and remembers Durrell's laughter as keynoting the summer. Perlès says it was a marvelous summer: wine and words flowed. The young Durrell seemed to him "a ball with the face of an angel." [8]

Perlès at this time was "playing" with a magazine called *The Booster*, turned over to him by a friend but actually owned by the American Country Club in Paris. Miller, Durrell, Perlès, and their friends completely subverted the magazine, and after three perky issues in which they largely promoted their own works and ideas, the magazine was repudiated by the president of the American Country Club. A fourth (the last) issue appeared, known as the "Air-Conditioned Womb" number because of Miller's contribution. *The Booster* was followed by *Delta* (three issues), which disappeared at Easter, 1939, with the "Peace and Dismemberment Number with Jitterbug-Shag Requiem." [9]

Durrell spent some time not only in Paris with Miller but also in London, where he began to know people and to be known. He met T. S. Eliot and found him "a very charming person"(118). But in 1938 Durrell returned to Corfu, where he built a house, wrote poetry, painted water colors, brooded, and matured. The mood of this period is caught and fixed in *Prospero's Cell*.

A reunion of the friends occurred in Paris in late 1938, and then Perlès and Durrell went to London, where Durrell, not yet reconciled to English ways, discovered he was becoming "literary." In the spring Miller visited Corfu, as his first stop on a projected trip to Tibet. He lingered at Corfu and never went to Tibet. Later Miller wrote about his Corfu and Greek excursion in *The Colossus of Maroussi*.[10]

Now enter the names of Greek friends: the "colossus," who is George Katsimbalis; and George Seferiades, who is better known as Seferis and who was recently catapulted to fame with a Nobel prize. Durrell's *Prospero's Cell* and Miller's *Colossus* both describe memorably the Greek world as found and cherished by sympathetic visitors like Durrell and Miller—under the shadow of impending war, but full of grace, generous laughter, and wit.

Miller responded joyfully to Corfu, a sea-and-sun world in which Durrell and his wife Nancy cavorted like glorious dolphins. Miller and Durrell also explored the mainland together. The time was late, however, and the Greek interludes were soon to be terminated by war. For a while Durrell taught at the British Institute in Athens. When the school closed, Durrell went to Kalamata, from which place he wrote Miller in November, 1940: "Ah Lao-tse, we need you here!"(168). In April of 1941 the Durrells escaped to Crete via caïque. After a short time in Crete Durrell went to Egypt to "serve" in the British Information Office in a job probably much like Darley's in the *Quartet* after Darley's return to Egypt. During the war, Durrell's wife and baby daughter Penelope Berengeria went to Palestine.

This period was one of emotional intensity and crises. Durrell's marriage had ended, but Durrell the professional writer went on working. Miller wrote to tell him that Durrell's poems were being praised, that he was being compared to Donne and Blake(172). Miller, settled in California, had now found his own style of living as well as writing.

Durrell became Press Attaché in Alexandria. In February, 1944, he wrote to Miller that he was "halfway through a book about Greek landscape—Corfu only." He was absorbing Alexandria, however, while writing about Corfu(181). His keen and increasingly intense impressions of Alexandria foreshadowed the transfiguration of this material into legend and myth in *The Alexandria Quartet*. Durrell in his early thirties in Egypt, already saddened by personal problems and sensitized by war, was unburdened by a university education and its frequent indoctrinations in methods of inquiry which exalt consistency. He developed his talent as an offering, not as a proof. He wrote almost proudly to Miller: "The poetry I exude these days is dark grey and streaky, like bad bacon"(187). He smelled the "atmosphere of sex and death" and revealed his excitement *and* despair. He met a "strange, smashing, dark-eyed woman . . . with every response right, every gesture, and the interior style of a real person, but completely at sea here in this morass of venality and money"(189). Such a woman perhaps exists only in a writer's imagination. It is no doubt best not to identify the women in Durrell's life with the women in his writing, but the temptation is great: Durrell has had three wives, and Darley three women. Durrell's fantasies, he told Miller, included the dream of going to an island with this wonderful dark lady.

In the spring of 1944 Durrell wrote to Henry Miller: "I have really grown up now and have plenty to say." He felt the urge to detach himself from the world: "The world has walls of dung really, and the human being a mind like a sponge. The next ten years should see us in full cry over the hills. Simple needs this time. A girl, an olive tree, a typewriter, and a few great friends like you. What do you think?"(190).[11]

Durrell is, of course, a *romantic*. And so is Miller. No wonder people beat paths to their doors in Big Sur or little Provence, and no wonder travel bureaus are constantly asked to find the Alexandria which Durrell created. These men, pioneers themselves and admirers of other pioneers such as Lawrence, Céline, and Lao-tse, weave dreams for little people. That they often put up with primitive sewage systems and eat perhaps too many olives and figs for efficient digestion is only what they must pay for their leadership and professionalism. In a word, Durrell was now ready to begin writing seriously. He had become, despite his diversity and complexity and multi-skills, an integrated person, a modestly arrogant representative of the kind of freedom which requires talent and guts (and at least a little money), and which the subscribers to escape magazines like to read about, and to imitate gently now and then—at a higher level of comfort and convenience.

In the spring of 1945 Durrell informed Miller that he was waiting to leave Alexandria to go to Rhodes, where he would become a "public information officer." He was working busily, and he mentioned a "new version of the Book of the Dead." Publications soon to come included *Cities, Plains, and People* (poems); *Prospero's Cell;* and *The Dark Labyrinth.* He was also interested in "a cabalistic group" and mentioned a Mr. Baltazian whom he intended to visit. (Scholars may note the resemblance of the name to Balthazar.) He was seriously interested in the esoteric, in the function of symbols, and in the Tarot. And his interest and respect led him to further definition of his "heraldic universe" and "nonassertive form"(201-04).

Much of his theorizing was nonsense, but the kind of no-sense that tried to articulate the ineffable. This aspect of Durrell may seem strangely naïve only to those who are ingenuously sophisticated. Astrology, Zen, and "pure apprehension" are literary modes. There is no need to test them theologically or philosophically.

Miller and Durrell invented magic for our time and made it fashionable, although like other moments of truth, it is easily debased. Miller's dream of China and Tibet, Durrell's dream of the heraldic universe, and their combined belief in the possibility of sainthood and freedom are aspects of their dedication to writing —and, in that context, professional and objective. Durrell's admiration for the minor psychologist Groddeck, for example, has baffled some of his followers; for Groddeck's "truth" was largely intuitive and less important than either Freud's or Jung's. Yet Durrell's vision of Groddeck's work was clear and compelling.[12]

Durrell, in his early thirties at the end of the war, was "liberated from his Egyptian prison and free at last to return to Greece," according to George Wickes in *A Private Correspondence*(207). Egypt may have been a kind of prison, but one apparently not so confining as Latin America and Yugoslavia would be later; for out of that "Egyptian prison" experience came much of the peculiar essence of the *Quartet*.

After Egypt came Rhodes, where for almost two years Durrell was "Director of Public Relations, Dodecanese Islands." This properly romantic period may be read about in *Reflections on a Marine Venus*. To Miller, Durrell wrote: "Not exactly Governor of these twelve islands, but damn near"(210).

Durrell now became increasingly aware of his writing as art, and he was searching for his style. In May, 1946, he was considering doing a verse play about Sappho. At that time his job ended on Rhodes, and about that time he married for the second time. He married the dark lady.

Two interludes followed: one as "Director," British Council Institute, Cordoba, Argentina (for about a year); the other, as "Press Attaché," in Belgrade, Yugoslavia. Durrell's experiences in officialdom gave him material for the humorous sketches which have embarrassed his ardent and too-serious admirers who want him to be more Joyce than Wodehouse. But Durrell *uses* all his experience. For example, his lectures on literature in Argentina were transformed into the *Key to Modern Poetry*. And out of the Yugoslavia interlude came the not-easy-to-place thriller, *White Eagles Over Serbia*.

His unhappiness in Argentina and Yugoslavia is on record. He hated Argentina for not being Greece; he hated Yugoslavia for its communism and poverty. While in Yugoslavia he violently rejected Miller's new work, *Sexus,* first in a letter in September, 1949, in which he referred to the "moral vulgarity" in the work and then in a terse telegram: "SEXUS DISGRACEFULLY BAD WILL COMPLETELY RUIN REPUTATION UNLESS WITH-DRAWN REVISED . . ."(266).

Miller was gracious, and Durrell relented; but the crisis, although it did not destroy the relationship, changed the emotional balance of the literary friendship so that it became now more friendship and less literary. Miller had proved his compassion by not getting angry, and Durrell had proved his loyalty by daring to criticize negatively. Durrell is a decent critic, and his impulse was probably as honest as it was uncharacteristic of a courteous person. But it is generally thought that from this time on Durrell was no longer a disciple.

The point is hardly worth the bother, however; for, although the "crisis" is a neat climax in *A Private Correspondence* as a book, it was not the significant event that the *discovery* of Miller was. Durrell never *undiscovered* Miller. As a matter of fact, *Sexus* was much less important than *Tropic of Cancer*, partly because it came later. Timing does matter, and the *first time* is still an event incomparably more important than subsequent times in a *breakthrough.* One can't go on breaking through. Once one is through, one is through.

III   *The Writer*

In January, 1950, Durrell wrote to Miller that he had been reading Stendhal, and a little later he reported that he had read Eliot's *The Cocktail Party*. He praised Eliot's "gentleness and humour and lovability"(282). Durrell, who had now completed his verse play, *Sappho,* was planning big things. In July he boasted that he had material enough "to furnish a dozen big novels." He was hopeful: "Next step is to buy a small house with the acre of land"(283). First, however, he had to spend approximately one more year in Yugoslavia. Then in December, 1952, he told Miller that he was about to set off for Cyprus: "No money. No prospects. A tent. A small car." He added: "I feel twenty years younger"(291).

This time there was no compromising. The Durrell in Cyprus is the Durrell of *Bitter Lemons*. He bought a stone house and began to teach English to Cypriots. Perlès, commenting on the collapse at this time of Durrell's second marriage, says Durrell was literally left "holding the baby." With the advent of the Cypriot conflict, he went to work in Nicosia as a press adviser. There he became "Public Relations Officer."

The Cyprus period, which continued on into August, 1956, was the most complete—in the sense of consummated—episode in that aspect of Durrell's life which is the proper concern of the student of literature. At age forty Durrell found himself "working" many hours a week—not writing! These hours were time lost. The situation was critical. The few left-over hours had to be made to count. He was *with book* and had to prepare for the birthing. First, he bought a small Turkish house. In November, 1953, he outlined his routine at that time to Miller as including thirty hours of teaching weekly and a commuter's round-trip to Nicosia daily. He enjoyed home ownership. His response to Cyprus as a place was almost religious. And he was reading the letters of Rimbaud.

By the fall of 1955 he reported that he was about half finished with *Justine:* "I believe it is very good"(302). He was also studying Zen Buddhism, via "Suzuki," while the political unrest on the island began to develop into a revolution. It added up: Rimbaud, Zen, "Eve's Alexandria," Cyprus—a great work was in the making.

By the summer of 1956 *Justine* was finished. The entrance in his letters to Miller of a woman called Claude (eventually to become his third wife) is quiet and reassuring. Durrell had found some security at long last. And in the fall of 1956, he left Cyprus to go to Dorset, where the natives reminded him of characters out of Thomas Hardy. There he worked on *Bitter Lemons*.

It all fits together: each place was material for a book to be written in the next place while getting material for the next book to be written in the next place. From Tibet to England to Corfu to Greece to Egypt to Rhodes to Latin America to Yugoslavia to Cyprus to Provence, with interludes in England and Paris: Durrell's itinerary now seems a wisely determined instead of adventitious one, with sufficient Levantine contrast, Greek austerity, and Slavic and Latin relief—backdropped by the memory, now a dream, of Tibet and reinforced with the hatred of that which was hateful in England.

In a cottage lent to him in Dorset, Durrell wrote *Bitter Lemons* in six weeks. The move to Provence which followed also coincided with a time of rigorous work. The schedule (Durrell was allegedly writing some fourteen hours a day for extended periods of time) resulted in *Balthazar* being written in six weeks; *Mountolive*, in twelve; and *Clea*, in eight! [13]

The *total* time it takes to write a book is, of course, *all* the time it takes the author to get where he is when he finishes the book by putting it down on paper. Nevertheless, one is astounded at such work habits. Inevitably, as soon as Durrell's amazing timetable was made public, critics sought—and found—evidences of slipshod writing. There were errors due to sloppy proofreading, but nothing else can be proved.

Out of the Provence years (Claude and Durrell were married, according to the *New York Times,* March 27, 1961) came the contemporary and almost legendary Durrell. Now increasingly successful, he had to protect himself from the curious and the fervent. The *Quartet* was launched. It caught on—in the United Kingdom, in America, on the Continent. Durrell's home in 1960, as described by British novelist Nigel Dennis, was "a place of pilgrimage." [14]

In the early 1960's Durrell appeared primarily as dramatist. Three of his verse dramas were performed: the earlier *Sappho,* then *Acte,* and finally *An Irish Faustus*—all at Hamburg's Deutsches Schauspielhaus. His dramas, especially the last two, have generally not been enthusiastically received.

As late as 1958 Durrell still acknowledged Miller and Eliot as "guides and mentors"—Miller "for or rather by example, and Eliot for advice"(343). Many other of his "sources" have yet to be identified. Source studies generally start with a dulled Occam's razor. Major and minor influences inevitably line up in complicated patterns behind the performances of even relatively uncomplicated people.

It is not possible to neatly resolve the biography of a contemporary. Just as Durrell ended *Justine* with "Workpoints and Consequential Data" in order to dramatize potentialities, so the account of this Irish Faustian who has been content with "a girl, an olive tree, a typewriter and a few great friends" also ends in potentialities. There is more to come.

CHAPTER 2

The Poetry

THERE is no easy order to the story of Durrell's career. To date, *The Alexandria Quartet* dominates; however, it is convenient to put Durrell's work as poet and as "lesser" novelist on record before wrestling with the spectacular tetralogy. Then, to avoid unnecessary repetition, Durrell-as-humorist, Durrell-as-travel-writer, and Durrell-as-dramatist are discussed after Durrell-as-novelist.

Classifying items as *major* or *minor* is an inevitable consequence of dealing with the extensive production of an active creator. And Durrell has been almost extravagantly prolific. He has been writing both casually and intensely for many years. His *minor* works are legion, but all works discussed in this study are relatively *major;* and their presence indicates, therefore, a judgment upon them as also *significant.*

I A Key to Modern British Poetry

When Durrell was attached to the British Council in Argentina in 1948, he delivered a series of ten lectures on "modern poetry" which were reprinted in 1952 as *A Key to Modern British Poetry.* The lectures are concerned with the twentieth-century poets whose "new voices" and "new signatures" were changing the sound and texture of poetry in the 1920's and 1930's.

Durrell's usual modesty, which disclaims pretense to scholarship, is appropriate to his objective: "how to persuade people to become their own contemporaries." [1] His enthusiasm, however, is not irresponsible. Durrell acknowledges his debts to Wyndham Lewis, Edmund Wilson, and Groddeck. [2] His thinking, he notes, has been influenced by anthropologists, psychologists, and scientists. Durrell is always informed—even if his information is not quite systematically filed.

Durrell's own poetry is contemporary in the sense that it is aware of and responds to other poets like Auden and Eliot. While reaching for its own voice, it has broken with neither history nor the *now*. Just as *contemporary* is only the moment *after* the last moment and *before* the next one, so modern poetry refers itself to both the past and to the future. The reading of any *current* poetry of value takes an informed reader; and essays such as Durrell's, which try to "disintoxicate" the readers with the *past* past, are worthy. For Durrell's objective is to "clear away much of the pedagogic lumber which accumulates insensibly in minds brought up in the traditions of scientific rationalism"(x).

The first "lecture" defines the limitations of critical methods and contrasts two poems, Tennyson's *Ulysses* and Eliot's *Gerontion* (written in 1840 and 1920, respectively). Between these two poems, Durrell contends, ideas about Time and the ego changed significantly. And what changed and how what changed affected poetry are the substance of the book. It can be summarized quickly as the switch from *believing* in the logical causality of an ordered universe in which time marched forward and the self was a stable, moral entity, to *believing* in only probability distributions of events in a relatively indeterminant universe. The result is an increase in the instability of self, the emergence of the relativeness of *all* moralities, and the consequent advent of the *artist* as a moralist. The break-down in the personality and ego-structure of ordinary man has given the poet a new strength and a desire to reach non-desire. The liberation of both scientist and poet is imminent, and the mystic road to wisdom may prove to be the same as the scientific road to knowledge. A "new reality" is at hand—the old securities have given way. In one of the lectures Durrell asserts: "Time and the ego are the two centres of focus for all contemporary poets with any pretensions to message"(83). Truth is apprehended only obliquely, through "nonattachment." The works of Aldous Huxley and Somerset Maugham, identified by Durrell as propagandists for this "nonattachment," correlate with the poems of Auden, Spender, Eliot, and Edith Sitwell. Finally the charm of all this theory about nonattachment and non-theory is that it floats free of space coordinates. In a deliberate and curiously orderly muddle of metaphysics and metaphors, it abdicates attempts even to understand itself.

II *Heraldic Reality*

It is usual to assume that if "B" equals "A," and if "C" also equals "A," then "B" equals "C." But in space-time it may not be so, for there traditional logic is inadequate. The classical syllogisms have omitted the time dimension and are thus fallacies.

In the traditional classroom when "X" equals "2," "2X" equals "4." In space-time it does not! Logic and algebra—which is the sign language of logic—require faith that shifts in time, and space positions do not affect the similarities involved. Substituting the second "X" for the first "X" in the simple equations above is a precarious event in space-time, for the sets of coordinates which define the first "X" and the second "X" are not the same. For example, the second "X" came later and is in a different place. The second "X" is different. In space-time, each symbol plays a unique, non-substitutable role.

The "heraldic aspect of reality" is that aspect of it which will not yield to algebraic manipulations without disaster—that is, without significant alterations. It predicts space-time concepts. The stupid child who had learned to add "X" and "X" to get "2X" was quite right when he refused to add "Y" and "Y" because he had not had "Y" yet. His suspicion that "Y" might behave differently from "X" honors the uniqueness of each experience; it also resists abstraction, generalization, and the other distortions of reality called for by algebra. In contrast to logic and algebra, the "heraldic design" does not *describe* the universe, does not try to represent it point by point.

Durrell, in a little essay reprinted in *Personal Landscape,* specified "unreason" as opposed to "causality" as the essential nature of this reality which the artist is trying to *see.* " 'Art' then is only the smoked glass through which we can look at the dangerous sun." [3] The dangerous sun is "heraldic reality," which is difficult to verbalize because words in sentences must be apprehended as ordered in time. They come *one after another.*

In *The Alexandria Quartet* Pursewarden refers to the heraldic concept in his "Notebooks." To reach the heraldic universe, he says, one must "leap": "Whoever makes this enigmatic leap into the heraldic reality of the poetic life discovers that truth has its own built-in morality!" [4] The heraldic design is the only *real* design, and it is not perceivable through any method that relies on causality, correlation, or algebraic substitutions. Mystically perceived truth, coming as it does without syntax (heraldry has *categories* only), is essentially heraldic. To Durrell, poetry is heraldic in that its symbols are non-algebraic and its existence is immediate.

III Collected Poems

Poetry usually falls between systematically controlled and spontaneously randomized writing. A poem is a kind of accident, with a low probability of its occurring at all and a high probability of its failing even when it occurs. Syntax in ordinary English is largely a matter of sequence. Poems, however, even in English, are more nearly ideograms—or heraldic devices—than prose. Although they must make some sense, the sense may transcend the syntax. Completely randomized verbalizations are nonsense (the language of schizophrenia), but *they* may be *accidentally* glorious—never on purpose. Poetry, however, must be *accidental on purpose;* and it hits its level of sense only by not fearing nonsense.

Durrell takes his poetry seriously, and it may well be his critical experiment in posterity's final evaluation of his work. Some of his poems are almost obscure. Many are lightly touched with humor or satire, but they are always tightly wound. The rhyme, if any, is approximate, obvious, or conventional. The rhythmic and stanza patterns vary, play on expectation, exploit the familiar, or parody the trite.

It takes a nimble reader to handle the required awareness of these subtleties without making *them* the substance of the poetic experience. Explication is often hostile, even fatal, to the kind of poetry that *needs* explication; for, the more crying the need for translation into understandable (i.e., more familiar and more nearly predictable verbal sequences), the more disastrous to original form such translation becomes. Joyce knew that his *Ulysses* needed to be *rewritten* in foreign language equivalents rather than translated. Fortunately, some of Durrell's poems comment on poetry; some are the near-equivalents of other of his poems; and *they* tend to explicate either themselves or the more difficult ones.[5]

Durrell has admired many poets, and the sources of his creations are sometimes artfully concealed, sometimes equally artfully revealed in the works themselves. But to tease out the variables —to subject the relatively innocent poems to fingerprint and footprint tests to discover who has been there and whose hand or foot lay heavy or lightly on form, texture, or pattern—is a kind of game often too violent for Durrell's poetry. Nevertheless, his poetry does yield to lightly handled explication. (All quotes from Durrell's poetry in this chapter are from *Collected Poems*.[6])

Durrell admired the Alexandrian Cavafy's poetry[7] for a special quality:

> And here I find him great. Never
> To attempt a masterpiece of size—
> You must leave life for that. No
> But always to preserve the adventive
> Minute, never to destroy the truth
> Admit the coarse manipulations of the lie.   (157)

One may hazard that "adventive" in this poem refers to both the "second coming" (as in theology) and "not native to the environment" (as in biology). The *meaning* of the word in the context of the poem about poetry flashes across the statement, and it is reinforced with the *never* phrase that follows. But this is the *statement* of the flash—not the realization, not the flash itself. The "adventive minute" as experience is shy of its name, comes without gloss. The poem may be the gloss, but the minute itself never a poem.

Good poetry is seldom simple. Poetry confounds in order to make clear. Paradoxically, the "adventive minute" must be chosen carefully. In another poem, "River Water," Durrell alludes to painting, to forests, and to truth apprehended through painting— as a metaphor for the forest, which itself is a metaphor correlated with perception:

> The forest wears its coats
> of oil-paint as lightly can

> what only brush-strokes built,
> feather and leaf and spray,
> married by choice and plan.   (40)

The marriage, or merger, which is a basic idea in Durrell's theory of poetry, is controlled "by choice and plan" at a particular moment.

The search is always for the "Word Prime." The poem is only a makeshift, a confession of the need to confess that which cannot be properly confessed, a paradox in that its attempt to express denies the magnificent knowledge, non-verbal or pre-verbal, that silence speaks. In "Anecdote VII: at Alexandria" the act of saying or writing has been likened to "this little rubbing together of minimal words." The important metaphor follows:

> Much as in sculpture the idea
> Must not of its own anecdotal grossness
> Sink through the armature of the material,
> The model of its earthly clothing:
> But be a plumbline to its weight in space . . .
>
> The whole resting upon the ideogram
> As on a knifeblade, never really cutting,
> Yet always sharp, like this very metaphor
> For perpetual and *useless* suffering exposed
> By conscience in the very act of writing.   (116)

Now the statement and the doing of it come together, for the metaphor is more than explication, more than adornment. The explanation of *how* poetry works begins to work in itself as the metaphor takes hold. A poet may promise that his sonnet will outlast the marble to which it alludes, but he knows the test is not the boast. The poet's task is to avoid the kind of clarity which dies quickly, the cliché which is already dead, the kind of simplification which immediately becomes aphorism or quotation and dies of its own smoothness. He must avoid the heavy weight of content, the "anecdotal grossness" demanded by engineers as "armature" and by the dullards as bait. Content there must be, and "armature" too, but delicately balanced. The poem is the "ideogram" that can balance on the knife-edge without being cut in half.

The importance of "place" and "landscape" in the Durrell vision is definitive. The "poet's truth" concerns itself with the various relationships among logic, psychology, spirit, and geography. Put that way it seems a precious, overwrought business; but Durrell's concept of place defines poetic truth and often controls metaphors and metaphysics. He believes in the "god of place." [8] The spirit's "panic fellowship" is ubiquitous:

> Your panic fellowship is everywhere,
> not only in love's first great illness known,
> but in the exile of objects lost
> to context, broken hearts, spilt milk,
> oaths disregarded, laws forgotten:
> or on the seashore some old pilot's
> capital in rags of sail, snapped oars,
> water-jars choked with sand,
> and further on, half hidden, the fatal letter
> in the cold fingers of some marble hand.   (280)

Poetry is also style. Style, the poet says, is "Something like the sea . . . /Or the wind":

> But neither is yet
> Fine enough for the line I hunt.
> The dry bony blade of the
> Sword-grass might suit me
> Better: an assassin of polish.
>
> Such a bite of perfect temper
> As unwary fingers provoke,
> Not to be felt till later,
> Turning away, to notice the thread
> Of blood from its unfelt stroke.   (18)

Here, again, the saying and the doing are married. The search for the metaphor becomes the metaphor.

Poems occur in full awareness of relative failure. On the blade of a knife the ideogram is balanced, at the edge of nonsense, between the self and the not-self:

> Truth's metaphor is the needle,
> The magnetic north of purpose
> Striving against the true north

> Of self: Fangbrand found it out,
> The final dualism in very self,
> An old man holding an asphodel.   (151)

This "dualism" (truth as one apprehends it and as it *is* objectively) is in all poetry. Which is to say that poetry *is* ambiguity and hovers between clarity (predictability) and obscurity (completely unpredictable sequences of words, images, and figures). The poet always writes *about* poetry as he writes poetry, and always creates himself as he writes about himself; and the words fall or do not fall here and there in a chosen randomness. The poem as poetry is always literal, is always a record of itself.

Durrell's favorite image is the mirror.[9] Its aptness lies in its expectedness, its very triteness—its useful modesty in the midst of more ambitious imagery. And the image in the mirror is the *real* double, the other self, accepted without question: ". . . watch the mirror watching you"(39). Imagery always has to do with the echo, the scent, the shape, or the trace left behind or projected ahead; something impressed on the eye, ear, skin, nostril: "Scent like a river-pilot led me there"(19). A psychologist would say that the scent is the minimum redintegrating stimulus for the total recall.

"Time's inflexible quantum" (42) controls all too well, and the only way to make the unmeetable meet is to be another, to watch oneself watching one's double. It *is* done with mirrors: the poem is an illusion, only a try at truth. It is an ideogram which mirrors reality *in design* instead of *sequence,* an admission of failure which transcends failure in the deathlessness of the admission.

The cracked mirror and the dry inkwell are the metaphors of frustration, distortion, and futility. And sometimes the poet "moves through negatives" to his statement, telling how difficult it is to tell, vowing to try to tell, dealing in ruins or traces of what once was or in signs of what might have been. Greece, the Levant, the Aegean, and the eastern Mediterranean offer debris as well as immediate moments of stuff and sense, a combination of nostalgia, resignation, and sharp response to present sensations.

Durrell is not averse to the straightforward statement about experience. And there are poems in almost every form as well as mode, often built around an "adventive" moment or a focussed recollection of a segment of time projected onto a flat surface. The lengthier poems are frequently collections rather than extensions, and sometimes they appear to have been gathered together later by the poet.

Some poems are clearly personal, even autobiographical. "Conon in Exile" refers to three women who "have slept with my books"(125):

> They were only forms for my own ideas,
> With names and mouths and different voices.
> In them I lay with myself, my style of life,
> Knowing only coitus with the shadows,
> By our blue Aegean which forever
> Washes and pardons and brings us home.   (127)

The idea can be materialized or the material can be idealized in images which are the poet's ideas about the originally concrete. Many poets have wrestled with theory as well as poems, including the poets who probably most "influenced" Durrell; but a poet worth his salt has struggled out of theory or through theory or has worked always at the level of pre-theory toward the poetic statement. He finds his own truth, his own style, and his own voice in his poems.

Durrell's *poetic* statements are not necessarily more nearly valid than his prose statements. The references in the poems which seem to predict the *Quartet* are not necessarily *predictive*. For example, the Melissa of the several poems in which the name is used as a form of address seems related to the Melissa of the *Quartet*, but the *original* Melissa is lost to the critic for sure, buried in the pre-history of both prose and poetry. What is known of her either in poems or in prose is only artfully selected debris: the monuments to someone, perhaps, or the idea of someone.[10]

True, the poems become increasingly interesting the better one knows the other works of Durrell, but as poems rather than as facets. They are themselves significant and often highly successful, taking no second prizes, asking no condescension from admirers of the more spectacular prose.

"Cities, Plains, and People" moves from the poet's childhood in Tibet to "Pudding Island o'er the Victorian foam" where the poet "saw the business witches in their bowlers . . ."(201). There he learned that London was not for him. Experience with books, truth's paradoxes, Paris-time, word-experiments follow. The conclusion is innocently rhymed: "All rules obtain upon the pilot's chart/If governed by the scripture of the heart"(205).

The pre-Hamlet, pre-Faust *knowing* is poetic truth, and the image of the Way is proper poetry. The poet explores himself and his universe, senses "the space-time void." But the critic is sterile:

> Within his ant-like formalism
> By deduction and destruction steers;
> Only the trite reformer holds his own.   (215)

"Letters in Darkness" is denser, more perturbed:

> In clinic beds we reach to where
> All cultures intersect, inverted now
> By the hungry heart and jumbled out
> In friends or sculpture or kissing-stuff,
> Measured against the chattering
> Of gross primary desires, a code of needs
> Where Marxist poems are born and die perhaps.
>
> The white screens they have set up
> Like the mind's censor under Babel
> Are trying to keep from the white coats
> All possible foreknowledge of the enigma.
> But the infected face of loneliness
> Smiles back wherever mirrors droop and bleed.   (246-47)

In the *Paris Review* interview of 1959 Durrell opined that many poems of his "middle period" were "too corpulent." [11] This kind of comment casually generated in a polite conversation may or may not mean anything. Anyway, "corpulence" is a relative term. "Over-writing" is conceded by Durrell as one of his "major difficulties"—yet that *overness* is at the center of his poetic talent; and the poems which become lean through over-paring are also the result of overness. A poem *is* distortion—on purpose.

Speaking of over-writing, Durrell remarked: "It comes of indecision when you are not sure of your target. When you haven't drawn a bead on it, you plaster the whole damn thing to make sure." In the same interview Durrell said what many poets say, that the writing of poetry is good discipline: "Poetry turned out to be an invaluable mistress. Because poetry is form, and the wooing and seduction of form is the whole game." And then he added: "My interest in form might be—I'm talking seriously now, not modestly—an indication of a second-rate talent." [12] But the ranking of talents by the talented is a delicate business, at best, and there is something about the second-best when it ranks itself as second-best that makes it first rate. At least the vitality of the bawdy and satirical poems, such as "Ballad of Kretschemer's Types," "Ballad of the Oedipus Complex," "Ballad of Psychoanalysis," and "A Ballad of the Good Lord Nelson," is always first-rate. In these the desire *to say* is passionate and honest.

Of his poetry Durrell also said: "To write a poem is like trying to catch a lizard without its tail falling off." [13] It can be said of Durrell-as-poet what can be said of any good poet: sometimes the tail falls off (and one publishes anyway!) but often the poem is only the account of the experience of trying to catch the lizard without its tail falling off. The poem is the record of the search for the poetic experience.

Men like Durrell write honest poems, for they are honest searchers.

CHAPTER 3

The Lesser Novels

DURRELL'S first novel, *Pied Piper of Lovers,* an ingenuous work, now belongs to collectors—by whom it is valued as a rare item.[1] Published in 1935, its literary innocence is attested to by its failure to attract much attention other than a publisher's recommendation that Durrell's subsequent work be ascribed to a pseudonymous Charles Norden in order to wipe clean the little slate of non-fame. Durrell himself seems not to refer to his first work again after his modest admission to Miller in January, 1937, that he had written "a cheap novel." [2]

Pied Piper of Lovers is described by George Wickes as "an account of bohemian life in Bloomsbury." [3] Written in the days when Durrell was trying to make a living, the sale of this literary merchandise was an important event. It gave the reinforcement necessary for the young man to turn to writing as a *profession.* He began at once to work on his second novel, *Panic Spring,* which he finished at Corfu and published in 1937. *Panic Spring* is worth discussion, for it is the real *beginning* and is a better book than critics, who patronize early works, have implied.[4]

I Panic Spring

Panic Spring is an island book, in the tradition of Douglas' *South Wind.* Nepenthe, Douglas' island, is a version of Capri; Durrell's island, Mavrodaphne (black laurel), is almost a toy in comparison to Douglas' Capri. Mavrodaphne is owned by a wealthy eccentric and is peopled in the book with several tarrying travelers who have met there partly by accident, partly by pattern. Each has been invited to stay by Rumonades, the wealthy owner of the island. Each is given his own villa, and each searches for his identity through a "panic" spring (*panic* from *Pan,* who used to startle travelers with fear and awe, although himself often a gentle pastoral creature) and into summer. In the end, the island-pattern is broken by the death of the benefactor; and the visitors again become pilgrims or return to their homes. It is a simple story.

Christopher Marlowe, a gentle schoolmaster, is fleeing from the English death which is later described in Durrell's *The Black Book;* and his flight is conventionally motivated and traditionally told. Marlowe, en route to Greece, is diverted by the Greek Revolution. He makes contact with a mysterious boatman—with small, Pan-like feet—from whom Marlowe buys passage to the island. There he meets the other "guests" of Rumonades, a forlorn and eccentric millionaire, who lives alone in the big house he built for his lovely wife, Manuela. Manuela has deserted him. Marlowe meets Gordon, Walsh, Francis, and Dr. Fonvisin—also Rumonades and several natives, including a woman who cooks and cleans for him, a local-color policeman, and a couple of dirty but devout monks.

Mavrodaphne is dedicated to the sea and to the sun. It is a place to swim and to talk. Marlowe, a slight young man, is writing a philosophical essay. Walsh, another young man, lives with his friend Gordon and writes popular songs. (One of his current hits is called "To Be or Not To Be"!) Gordon is older, handsome, and well-off. Francis (a woman) is a painter. Although saddened by life, she is young enough to attract Walsh and to attract Marlowe to the idea of being attracted to her.

Gordon is the brother of Walsh's dead wife, Ruth. Walsh, in a backflash, is explained and motivated, *à la* Huxley, in episodes of decay and numbness. There is also mention of a schoolmaster named Tarquin and of a doctor named Trigger in Walsh's background—shadowy people who will take surer form in *The Black Book* and emerge multi-dimensional in the *Quartet*. Fonvisin, the physician on the island, is also shadowy—and shadowed. His drunkenness and his story-telling talent are utilized in "his chapter." The account of how he assisted in making a modern mummy is a worthy forerunner of the morbid and occult excursions in the *Quartet*. Moreover, Marlowe predicts Campion of *Cefalu* and Darley of the *Quartet* and by the same token suggests the novelist himself. His flight from England, his interest in systematic and philosophical quietism (grace through contemplation, wisdom through passiveness), and his obsession with words suggest also Lawrence Lucifer of *The Black Book.*

The *woman* Francis is the most complex character. She has run away from poverty and unhappy love on the mainland. She has some sort of illustrating job which she carries on part-time on the island, and she is worshipped by Rumonades, who has grown accustomed to her presence as surrogate for his wife. But she rejects all offers of love, smokes and paints and lies in the sun; she is searching herself for herself. She is a sort of preliminary draft of Clea in the *Quartet,* but then most women in general are only preliminary drafts of Clea!

Francis is given a long back-flash chapter which stops the book in midpassage. Gordon has no chapter of his own, perhaps because he has private means and thus less anxiety. In the end, after some good talk and some good listening to music and to the sea, Walsh stands at the top of "The Jump," a high cliff formerly used to test guilt or innocence of the accused. Survival after jumping means innocence; death, guilt. Walsh does not jump, however, and that evening the beginning of the end of the island interlude is put into motion. A farewell party for Francis precedes the death of Rumonades by a few hours. The panic subsides. The survivors leave.

Panic Spring is a put-together job by a young writer who is impressed by and borrows from the best talents and minds of his time. Durrell pretended little more then, and he certainly pretends little more now, about this novel.[5] It stands, however, on its own two feet: literateness and probity.

II The Black Book

References to Durrell's *The Black Book* as an "early" work have also tended to blur its significance. The fact of its earliness—Durrell was twenty-four when it was conceived, and he was responding intensely to Henry Miller's break-through in *Tropic of Cancer* —has positioned it as prelude to the *Quartet.*[6] It is more than that, however.

The 1960 American edition (a reprint) is burdened with two introductions, one by Gerald Sykes, one by Durrell himself.[7] Sykes sees the early work as predicting the *Quartet:* "All of his favorite colors are already spread out on the palette; they are

merely waiting to be put to mature use." But Sykes apologizes for
the four-letter words, calling them "a weakness." He feels Durrell
was "still too young to be naughty with style" (9).

The author is honest. In *his* prefatory statement, written almost
twenty-five years after the original work, he calls it "the genuine
article." It remains, he says, "a two-fisted attack on literature by
an angry young man of the thirties" (13). Originally, Durrell says,
he had not intended to publish the work. At that time he was
writing other (and publishable) stuff, but the enthusiastic response to the manuscript he sent to Henry Miller led to its publication in Paris in 1938 and to its discovery by critics like Cyril
Connolly and T. S. Eliot.

There are two narrators in *The Black Book:* Lawrence Lucifer,
who is telling of his former experiences at a run-down London
hotel (the Regina) and his life as a teacher from his perspective
of "now" on Corfu, and Herbert Gregory, the author of a diary
called *The Black Book,* found by Lucifer in a room of the hotel.
The two narrators deal with pretty much the same material and
the same characters in two different times. The resulting confusion is deliberate, for here are both the projections of action in
space (time controlled or annihilated) and the heraldic patterns
which intrigued the young writer and which led, solemnly or ironically, to the theoretical structure of the *Quartet.* Pretty much
anything that can be said about the effectiveness and ineffectiveness of Durrell's experimental techniques in the *Quartet* can be
said, on a much reduced scale, about *The Black Book.* However,
the reduction in the scale is a critical factor. Smaller scales are per
se less pretentious and arouse fewer suspicions.

Had Durrell not written the *Quartet, The Black Book* might
have remained obscure. Perhaps it is the sort of book that ought to
remain obscure; for, despite its lustiness, it is a fragile thing. The
characters, seen from the point of view of both the young Lucifer
and the middle-aged Gregory, are grotesques. Dusty and shifty,
they are loaded with adjectives and bright, tense phrases. They
tend to wither in the light of an explication or synopsis.

After a few paragraphs of color and line, light and shadow,
contrasting the Levantine background of the narrator with his
memories of London, Lucifer evokes his characters: Tarquin,
Clare, Lobo, Perez, Chamberlain, Gregory, Grace, Peters, Hilda.

[44]

These are not *really* characters. They are the "logic of personalities." As patterns and devices they will be projected—in space, out of time.

Gregory is a forty-year-old Englishman. Lobo and the others never quite understand either Gregory or Lucifer, nor do Gregory and Lucifer understand each other, for they never meet. According to his diary, Gregory has been interested in Chamberlain, who lives (tense in *The Black Book* is equivocal) or lived in a flat nearby with his wife and three dogs. Chamberlain often speaks of sex, "his manner closely modeled on the style of Lawrence's letters"(38). Gregory, who realizes that he himself is subject to flights of fancy writing, comments: "This is becoming fine writing in the manner of the Sitwells"(40). The judgment, however, is only a trick: the comment on the comment. Lucifer comments on Gregory, and the novelist comments on Lucifer's comment.

There is much talk of loneliness. Enter Gracie, the whore, ancestress of Melissa: "Gracie was bought, without any bargaining, for the promise of a cup of coffee . . ."(45). Gracie is dirty, and Gregory bathes her. She is ill, but she is honest. Gregory gives a party for her. Everyone comes. "Perez, the gorilla with his uncouth male stride and raving tie; Lobo agitatedly showing his most flattering half-profile; Clare, Tarquin, Chamberlain with his bundle of light music and jazz"(49-50). Gregory is exploiting Gracie, and the others are embarrassed. Later Gregory himself finds Gracie odious. Then Clare and Gracie go to bed together, and Tarquin and Gregory are both betrayed.

By this time one realizes that Durrell's writing is always more subtle than Henry Miller's. Durrell's intelligence, which keeps showing, gives him an almost bemused self-consciousness about his liberation from the past that Miller lacked. This difference may have helped cause the crisis between Miller and Durrell over Miller's *Sexus*—a book which Durrell thought in bad taste. *Sexus* takes itself too seriously.

Lucifer, as the "I" narrator, assumes little responsibility for his own contribution to the book, none for "Gregory's Diary." Durrell has put distance between himself and Gregory. Lucifer locates his narrative in space: "I live only in my imagination which is timeless . . ."(59). Gregory may include the time dimension in his diary; but, as the diary is used by Lucifer, it is a projected map rather than a chronology. And thus the hotel is peopled with ghosts who live not from then to now but are fixed in patterns.

Lucifer begins to tell about Morgan, the janitor, an heroic character, then breaks off, returns to Gregory's diary, in which Gregory is remembering Gracie. Then he returns to himself. Now working in a school, Lucifer carefully describes the schoolroom, remembers and confounds memories with perceptions. Soon sexual intercourse triumphs over time in a fervent passage which helps to give the book its purple, controversial tone (64).

Then he reverts to the hotel, to Tarquin, Clare, and trouble. Lucifer sighs: "The truth is that I am writing my first book. It is difficult, because everything must be included: a kind of spiritual itinerary which will establish the novel once and for all as a mode which is already past its senium" (69).

Gregory has not been able to do it—to include everything. He has tried to write a book called URINE, but only the title page has emerged. Gregory refers to Rimbaud, licks his lips on words, admits he is a liar. Then the narrative shifts back to Lucifer, who locates a given night "dimly." He tells of Connie, the brewer's widow; of Clare, Perez, and Hilda.

For Connie, Hilda, and others, Lucifer tries to compose an elegy, but they are all too elusive as people. Lucifer says: "The last tram has gone. The epoch from which this chronicle is made flesh, when I think of it, is an explosion. My lovely people like so many fragments of an explosion already in flight . . ." (92). Then Lucifer remembers a visit to the Chamberlains, writes of Tarquin, Morgan, Lobo. He concludes: "Words are no good. If you were to die, for instance, it would mean snow. Palpable, luminous, a shadow in ink" (99).

Then follows more talk of loneliness, of prostitutes, of artists: prostitutes and artists are alike, respect one another. Lucifer writes of the *English* death. And "Book One" closes with a "negus to the death of the world, to the snow, the calamity of whiteness, the doves, the harlots, the music." [8]

In "Book Two" the "school" is identified as *Honeywoods*. It is fixed in space, partially in time. This is where Lucifer "maunders" through his day's work. There Marney, a hunchback, teaches Spanish; Ohm, economics; Madame About, French. But most memorable of all is the student Miss Smith, a Negress, who is "working away at The Life and Times of Chaucer"(126). "I tell you," Lucifer exults, "when she reads the world moves into a dimension of pure sensation"(130-31). As Lucifer listens, the words turn into colors. He feels "the slow corrupt delirium of rebirth." And he asks himself, at the moment of Epiphany: "Is this amusia, aphasia, agraphia, alexia, abulia?" He answers: "It is life"(131). Henry Miller especially liked that part: the words, words, words!

Back at the hotel Lobo watches himself make love in the mirror. Lobo is always homeless: "The womb is his target, but he misses it. Something intervenes, a letter, a bill, a calculation, a fit of weeping, blood, nostrums, fear"(135). Lucifer has a good moment: "I gather your face up like a goblet of brandy and drink it solemnly, mouth, eyes, hair, nose, lips, canines, lobes, dimples, tics —everything in a gulp"(137).

In the middle of the work the novelist announces that his book is "a quarrel with destiny"(139). He is determined: "The important thing is this: if I succeed, and I will succeed, then I shall become, in a sense, *the first Englishman*"(141). After this intimate moment in the text, there is no way back to the detached irony of the early pages. The characters are further projected, confounded, illuminated, and finally fixed in space; but the burden of the book grows heavy.

Lucifer makes love to Chamberlain's wife, tells Tarquin about it. Of Hilda, he remembers her "great rufus vulva like a crowded marketplace; the great conduit choked with blood and paper and cigar ends which we must accept before we can go any farther" (166). The characters become "heraldic," fixed in their moments, attributes, and significances—like playing cards: "We were entering into a fiction, and all this is merely the paraphernalia of ballet, the insignia of clowns or swans strutting before some too stylized back-cloth. That is why this writing had to become ballet and ape it: not the emotion of personalities, but a theater of the idea. Ourselves, if we still had 'selves', as the projection of an idea tossed under a spotlight to spin and dither like Japanese waltzing mice . . ." [*sic*].(167)

Tarquin discovers he is homosexual. Lawrence Lucifer makes his will, bequeathing his soul to hell, his body to earth. Perez makes love, makes love, makes love (only he uses a simpler word for the function)—and he can't get enough. The fantasy continues in Hilda's womb, which has now become a whale.

In "Book Three" Gregory writes of his marriage to Gracie. Gracie begins to plan Gregory's life, beginning with the elimination of Tarquin, then Clare. The Chamberlains call less and less often. When Gracie dies her father comes to see the body, says, "Well, what's done's done"(199).

Tarquin starts to write a novel about Jesus. He turns Jesus into a woman. Gregory takes up with Kate, with whom he has nothing in common, to whom he has nothing to say. She will be his "sanctuary." Gregory makes his will, leaving bits of his personality to his friends. He himself intends to "sift gently into fragments" (217). Thus ends Gregory's diary, but Lucifer takes some thirty pages more to end his narrative. It is winter, and they have all made a truce. Tarquin, Lobo, Perez, and Lucifer talk of suffering. Chamberlain laughs as he reads a new magazine in the corner. Lucifer finally *understands* Chamberlain, but he had *admired* Gregory, the exile. Chamberlain is only a "colonizer." Lucifer is growing up. . . .

This summary is as incoherent as the original and without any of its charm, for one can't summarize a book that is not a book but a projection. Perhaps one could draw it, but one can't say what it says; for it says that what it has to say is virtually unsayable.

Phoebe Adams, in the *Atlantic Monthly*, wrote of *The Black Book:* "Mr. Durrell has since learned to translate his ideas into plot structure instead of tossing them into the story like the parsley on a fish platter." [9] That is to say, the projection of the work as heraldic design instead of chronological narrative seemed to the critic naïve and primitive. Durrell has, however, known how to tell a story (with or without parsley) all along; but he has not always wanted to. Perhaps plot structure (the patterning in time of selected events) is the relatively primitive technical device, not heraldry.

III   The Dark Labyrinth

Originally published as *Cefalû* in England in 1947 and reissued in America in 1962 as *The Dark Labyrinth*, this work is another "early" novel. Like *The Black Book* it has been the victim of condescension and misplaced enthusiasms. The book survived its first publication without much notice, and not until the success of the *Quartet* was it issued in America.[10] In 1945, in a letter to Henry Miller, Durrell described *Cefalû:* "It is really an extended morality, but written artlessly in the style of a detective story. Guilt, Superstition, The Good Life, all appear as ordinary people; a soldier on leave, a medium, an elderly married couple (Trueman), a young unfledged pair, a missionary. I have deliberately chosen that most exasperating of forms, the situation novel, in which to write it. I knocked it off in a month in order to hold my depression at bay." [11]

The young Durrell of the 1940's was fired with the awareness of his own potential. He knew that the excitement Miller's work created in him indicated that he too would ultimately experiment and originate. He was self-conscious about the similarities between his *Cefalû* and Huxley's novels, and he certainly was aware that the formula he was using was trite. His detached attitude toward the work was a defense—and healthy and informed.

The particular satisfactions in the novel come from the Durrellian sensibilities superimposed on an old formula. The novel owes much to Aldous Huxley, but it also has a voice of its own. Addressed to those who care, it takes its issues seriously. A safe interval above the thrillers that it rather deliberately imitates, it instructs while it entertains; and it always distinguishes between the two values.

Durrell's careful attention to the past histories of his characters reveals his conscience. He could not let the formula take over completely. Yet these attempts to give depth and dimensions to the characters almost sabotage the whole business by adding irrelevant details. Most of the characters, however, carry the burden of allegory gracefully. They are stereotypes, of course, for the demands of the morality control that aspect of characterization. Miss Dombey, the missionary, *is a missionary*—not much else. And Campion is the average of all brilliant and cynical artists.

The writing is professionally smooth. Durrell has learned his trade. In *Cefalû* he is using a conventional form that he can handle. He must get a cast of characters to set sail together, must get a group of them into the labyrinth—and some of them out again.

And he must make it all add up. The central metaphor, the labyrinth, takes the characters to Crete, and each of the seven major characters enters the labyrinth as part of his own search. The attitude of each toward the labyrinth and the degree of his anxiety shape the individual destinies.

Several characters, like the American reporter in the first scene, and Katina, the servant-wife, dangle; for they belong only to the story-framework which includes a prelude called "The Argument" and an epilogue called "At Cefalû." But no major character is not accounted for fully in the end. Some of the surprises—such as the fact that the hoax was *fixed* (the statues were really genuine) and that Axelos is married to his servant—are manipulated and heavy. Yet the novel ends with an authentic sigh.

The story is not easily summarized—nor should it be easy to summarize, for art is more devious and more complicated than life—but it is mainly concerned with a pleasure cruise. Those aboard the ship, called the *Europa*, include Lord Graecen, Captain Baird, Mr. Fearmax, Mr. Campion, Miss Virginia Dale, Miss Dombey, and Mr. and Mrs. Truman. These are the eight characters to "account for."

Lord Graecen, gentleman poet, has resigned his curatorship in the Graeco-Roman section of the British Museum in order to visit his friend, Silenus Axelos, in Crete. Axelos has found in the labyrinth an ancient temple complete with statues. The authenticity of the temple becomes a side issue. Graecen has been told by his doctors that he is about to die. As a known but insignificant poet he has loved publishing his verses, of which he has seven volumes to his credit.

Lord Graecen's psychoanalyst friend, Hogarth, a good talker, has introduced him to Captain Baird. Baird, also sailing on the *Europa*, is going to Crete in order to dig up the body of a German prisoner of war he had to shoot. He is intent on expiation and absolution.

Another patient of Hogarth's, and a fellow passenger on the *Europa*, is the famous medium Fearmax. He has been "doctoring" since he lost his beloved familiar spirit, French Marie; and he is vaguely in search of his lost spirit and his lost health. He also wants to visit the Great Pyramid.

Another fellow traveler, Miss Dombey, known to John Baird

when he was a youngster (another coincidence), awaits the Second Coming; and she passes out pamphlets appropriate to her faith. She is all that the formula requires of the spinster traveler, complete with dog and acid tongue.

Virginia Dale, typist at the Ministry of Labor, simple, sweet, and attractive, is traveling for her health—and is discovered by Graecen trying to decipher one of Graecen's anthologized poems as part of her study for a "certificate." Graecen, in a world apart from the simple girl, responds to her request for help and is on the point of asking her to marry him when the catastrophe in the labyrinth occurs.

Campion, an unorthodox and intense painter, small of stature, is coolly articulate and "permanently in revolt" (65). Joining the cruise at Marseilles, he is on his way to Crete to do a job for the "War Graves people." He has just left his mistress. Baird, who has met him at cocktail parties in London and in the war, does not like him. But Lord Graecen admires Campion's paintings.

The Trumans, middle-aged, winners of the cruise in a magazine contest, are determined on enjoyment.

A series of patterns, mostly tenuous and coincidental, relate the characters to one another. Fearmax and Baird have had the same psychoanalyst. Campion has long admired Fearmax's articles on reality and the astral states. Graecen is a friend of Fearmax's and Baird's psychoanalyst; and Baird has known Miss Dombey for years. The Trumans are at first unrelated and uncommitted to the other passengers, but aboard ship Mrs. Truman sleeps with Campion and he paints her picture.

Not on the cruise, but passive agents in the action are Axelos and Hogarth. Axelos' home, Cefalû, is near the labyrinth and the village. He is Graecen's friend, and the discoverer and fake-forger of the genuine New Era antiquities in the labyrinth. Hogarth is a psychoanalyst whose wisdom complements Axelos' cynicism.

Warned against visiting the labyrinth as unsafe, the figures in this morality nevertheless sign up for the excursion. After viewing the antiquities and hearing the "roar of the minotaur," the party is ready to leave the underground maze of passages when the guide causes an extensive cave-in by climbing for partridge eggs. The guide is killed.

Miss Dombey, trapped in a passage and without a flashlight,

uses up her supply of matches one by one; but she finds no way out. Swallowing a bottle of sleeping pills she apparently always carries with her, she sinks into her pre-death trance muttering a prayer which asks God why she has never believed in Him. So much for the missionary, who finds in the labyrinth that the Second Coming is her own death.

Fearmax, the mystic, lasts a little longer. He pursues down intricate passageways, following the smoke from his cigar—the hysteria-produced vision of his lost spirit, French Marie, and also the fetid odor of the minotaur. Coming to a crossroads in the passages, he follows not the smoke, which might have led him out, but the odor of the beast; and he gives himself up to the minotaur, whatever it may be. But Graecen escapes almost immediately by stumbling into a back passage which leads up and out, in sight of Axelos' house.

Baird, who went to dig up his German soldier instead of entering the labyrinth, spends time with Abbot John, a brigand priest and a former companion in arms, who has wisely concealed from Baird the fact that he himself has already dug up Böcklin, the dead soldier, and given him decent burial in the church. Baird finds nothing when he digs—an apparent miracle. Thus his guilt is exorcised.

Campion and Virginia Dale manage after the cave-in to climb out onto a balcony-like ledge in the face of a sheer cliff overlooking the sea. Joy at escape yields to dismay when they see there is no way to scale the cliff, up or down—no handholds and no footholds. Campion throws Miss Dombey's dog over the edge of the ledge. The dog survives the fall into the ocean, so Virginia and Campion decide to jump—in the morning: then, stripped naked, they take the plunge. Symbolism and allegory! Virginia is rescued from the ocean later, but Campion can not swim. He is lost.

The Trumans, rationing their frugal lunch, set forth to find a way out with reasonableness and resignation. They finally emerge into the open, into a lost-horizon-land, the "roof of the world," which is a pastoral, fertile plain ringed with mountains. But there is no exit. In this lost land they meet an American woman, Ruth Adams, who has found peace there years ago and has not tried to find her way back through the labyrinth.

Ruth Adams, slightly more than the standard philosophical survivor of worldly turbulence, has much to say about life; and it is all good and sound. Finally the Trumans accept their lostness too. Parachutists inadvertently have dropped much German war equipment on the plateau, so fortunately there is no lack of blankets and trousers and other necessary things.

Analogues and archetypes galore exist for this kind of plot, and its charm consists in Durrell's unabashed use of the device *once more*. What the Trumans find, as the result of isolation from the pre-labyrinth world, is repose. As Ruth Adams explains it to Elsie: "It's rather a negative business—becoming still enough inside to be receptive to it. You can't seek for it, but if you prepare for it it will come and settle on you like an Emperor moth. In fact, not 'seek and ye shall find' as the Bible says, but 'prepare and ye shall be found.' Oh, I can't hope to make it any clearer" (245).

In contrast, Graecen near the end of the novel says sadly: "We live in a rational world. . . . I suppose everything has a rational explanation" (260). Graecen stays in the rational world and is sad about it. Elsie Truman discovers the world of the imagination, one above the rational, on the roof of the world; and she is glad to stay there.

All but the guilt-obsessed Baird entered the labyrinth, and each found what he was destined to find. What to make of Baird is not quite clear, for he and Abbot John seem to have settled things pretty well outside the labyrinthian exploration of the self. The other "fates" are definitive. Fearmax and Miss Dombey come to the most violently futile ends. Campion's leap to freedom would have succeeded if he had known how to swim. Virginia's innocence saves her, perhaps—although she does break a leg. Graecen escapes the disaster to die the death predicted for him by his fashionable London doctors; but then the death rate is always one hundred per cent, so his fate is also the fate of every man.

Axelos and Hogarth remain outside the events. Axelos pretended to forge what was genuine. He is a god. Hogarth is a savior. To Miss Dombey and Fearmax, the minotaur was a fearful beast. To the Trumans, who *saw* it, a gentle cow. To Axelos and to Graecen—a boy hired to blow a horn into an opening to the caves! In the end Graecen sighs; he says to his friend Silenus Axelos: "I'm only sorry about the minotaur" (263).

Durrell wrote this novel quickly, but there is much in it that reflects the best in the Durrell quest for truth. It deals with knowledge beyond the systematically knowable. Despite its derivative qualities, it is authentic Durrell and rings true.

IV White Eagles Over Serbia

The raw materials and the scenic backgrounds of Durrell's only "juvenile" are more than incidentally excellent. They come from his Yugoslavian period. First published in 1957, *White Eagles Over Serbia* is a strange sibling to *Justine,* also first published in 1957. According to the implications of a note in Potter and Whiting's *Checklist,* Durrell himself identified the work as a "juvenile" only when his publisher did so.[12]

Durrell, a thoroughly professional writer by the 1950's, had planned to make money with this kind of story—but he apparently failed to get such items easily published. As a professional, he did not object to his work being marketed as a book for teenagers, but certainly as such it is a subordinate—although respectable—item in the Durrell canon.

To adults there's often something rather embarrassing about books for young readers. Perhaps the embarrassment is related to the condescension involved—one way or another. Either the writer condescends to the reader, or the critic condescends to the writer. Graded reading matter is associated with the educational system which developed as a function of intelligence testing, which in turn depends upon the concept known to educators as "mental age." Presumably the readers of this work will be between fourteen and eighteen mental-years old. Interestingly enough, one reviewer thought parents might object to some of the action which includes violent deaths of people and animals. At the same time adults might admire the "poetic pictures of the Serbian uplands." [13]

The story of *White Eagles* is predictable. Colonel Methuen, veteran British agent, impassioned fly-fisherman, and admirer of Thoreau, goes to Belgrade disguised as an Embassy accountant. The adventures of Colonel Methuen include an involvement with a girl named Vida—who is working for both "them" and "us"—and an encounter in their mountain hideout with Black Peter and the White Eagles, an outlaw royalist organization.

Colonel Methuen, disguised as a peasant, tramps the back-

ways, fishes, meditates, wrestles with the problems created by political realities and exigencies, and participates in the climactic
battle between the "good guys" and the "bad guys." The ambush
scene, in which the White Eagles lose the treasure they hoped
would finance the overthrow of Tito, is the moment of greatest
intensity in this professionally intensified story.

The verbal dexterities of a good writer do not falter because he
is intent on being intense, but somehow a larger proportion of
clichés may result from the attempt. In the midst of the finely
timed action and effective settings in a country which Durrell
knew and responded to, one finds that Methuen is often in a
"fever of impatience" or capable of a "sudden shudder." However,
Tito's Communist dictatorship of Yugoslavia is superior subject
matter, and the mountains of Serbia are unusually original material as setting, so that, despite its traditional structure and tone,
the story is engaging at a remarkably cliché-free level.

CHAPTER 4

The Alexandria Quartet *as Story*

FAME and prosperity came to Durrell with the publication of the tetralogy known as *The Alexandria Quartet*. Since the work was conceived as an experiment, as a "space-time novel" and not as a series of four stories, it is best considered as one unit. The parts of this "four-decker," however, were originally published separately between 1957 and 1960 as *Justine, Balthazar, Mountolive,* and *Clea.*

An analysis of such a complex creation as *The Alexandria Quartet* is a delicate exercise in assorting many variables. Thus three chapters of this study are given over to the *Quartet,* as the novels may be called for brevity. In this chapter the content of the work as story is reviewed. The next two chapters deal with the work as experiment and as "oracle"—that is, as a new form telling its own kind of truth. The following review of the narrative patterns may serve as a refresher of the numerous details and involved "plots" in the *Quartet;* for, without a basic vocabulary of the characters and the events, critic and reader cannot converse meaningfully about such an elaborately designed work. The *Quartet* is constructed in such a way that many of the major characters both observe and participate, and the narrative is complicated further by the introduction of letters, parts of journals, and many backflashes. Also, the theory of space-time fiction calls for intricacies and convolutions which make synopsis difficult. Although the conventional aspects of fiction such as story, plot, and characters are still Durrell's basic ingredients in his experiment, these ingredients are often confounded. The story-line is devious, even blurred; and the events are usually plotted in several dimensions. The result is literally intriguing. The *Quartet* defies humdrum methods of condensation. Yet the apparent obscurity yields to careful analysis. In the following book-by-book summary an attempt has been made to indicate the significant relationship of each major character to the other characters and to the story, and to fill in the background of each character at his first appearance in the work so that the summaries may be maximally useful as references.

I Justine

The first volume of the *Quartet*—each of the four parts may be thought of as a volume if the whole work is perceived as one novel—opens quietly. An unidentified narrator, living on an island in the Cyclades, is looking through some "papers" which evoke in him vivid memories. This important narrator is identified in the second volume as L. G. Darley, and he may conveniently be called "Darley" at once. As Darley reminisces about the past, the past becomes the present, and certain "facts" begin to emerge.

Darley is a poor Anglo-Irish schoolteacher. He is pleasant, unassuming, and neither young nor old. Later in the story he works as a minor official in the War Office in Alexandria. Although his initials are the same as Durrell's and at times his background resembles his creator's, Darley is not Durrell; for Durrell does not relinquish his proper role as novelist. Durrell's voice is always *more* than Darley's.

Darley is both a device and a character. As one of the novelist's devices for telling the story, he is a limited observer and reporter. As a character, he is a searcher for meanings; and in both roles his identifications remain uncertain for some time. To him, "all ideas seem equally good" in the beginning of the story (*J*:41).[1] But he is persistent in his search. He is the kind of man who goes to a whorehouse to *observe* the sex act: "I want to know what it really means," he says (*J*:185). Usually Darley is willing to alter his impressions of the "truth" as new evidence comes to his attention, but sometimes his respect for documents, some of which are unreliable, is ingenuous. Although the result does not make for straightforward narrative, he is a good rememberer, and he works hard at telling his tales.

The first volume of the *Quartet* is a memory book based on many sources. Darley refers to the diary of a wealthy Jewess, Justine Hosnani, which was given to Darley by Justine's husband, Nessim. Darley also refers to a child—the daughter of someone called Melissa—and to "Cohen's rings," which Darley has buried under the hearthstone. Darley remembers pre-war Alexandria and the beginnings of his love affair there with Justine at a time when he was almost happy with Melissa, his prostitute-mistress.

Melissa, at the time Darley recreates her in his memory (she is "now" dead), is a dancer in a night club. She has just left an unpleasant old man, a furrier named Cohen, to live with Darley. Darley tells how he found Melissa "washed up like a half-drowned bird, on the dreary littorals of Alexandria, with her sex broken . . ." (*J:24*). Melissa Artemis—her last name has symbolic value—is a gentle creature, loyal to those who are kind to her. Her devotion to Darley is only one of her "many faces." When she dies of tuberculosis, Darley refers to her dead face as "the last term of a series" (*J:238*). In one way or another she is friend to and is befriended by the other major characters in the *Quartet*. Eventually her personality touches them all. When, in the last volume, Darley realizes that he has begun to forget Melissa, he asks himself: "Was she simply a nexus of literary cross-references scribbled in the margins of a minor poem?" (*C:41*). One of the eighteenth-century Pamela's *fallen* daughters, Melissa is related to Hardy's Tess and to Dostoyevsky's Sonia. She is that romantic paradox invented by literature—a virtuous whore.

Like Melissa, Justine Hosnani leaves her mark on all four volumes. An authentic Alexandrian, beautiful and complex, Justine is a talented pianist, a discerning reader, a subtle lover. She is variously motivated—and even more variously described. Like Melissa, she has more than one "face," but the several aspects of Justine never quite fuse; for one of Durrell's techniques in this work is to avoid facile syntheses. Thus Justine's personality is deliberately elusive. First described as "sibling" to "giant man-eating cats" (*J:20*), Justine runs the gamut of many syndromes: lesbian, voluptuary, nymphomaniac, hysteric, somnambulist. She is called —even by herself—"the tiresome classical Jewess of neurology" (*J:149*).

Justine is impressionable: "A walking abstract of the writers and thinkers whom she had loved or admired" (*J:203*). She is surrounded by an aura of sexuality; and although in the fourth volume she appears to Darley as tawdry and over-perfumed, he has by that time changed more than Justine—and his perception is prejudiced. Justine never really loses her sexual attractiveness.

And as Darley recalls his first passion for her, she is gloriously haloed by his love. Others, of course, see her differently; but all agree about her sexuality. The least enthusiastic description finally comes from her most cynical lover, the novelist Pursewarden, who calls her "a tiresome old sexual turnstile through which presumably we must all pass" (*B*:115).

The definitive account of Justine's "life" is locked in the intricacies of the narrative technique as well as buried in the darker, secret aspects of Alexandria. Her background remains hazy. Born obscure and poor, Justine was raped early in life by a distant relative identified first only as a man wearing a black patch over his eye. Justine built the episode into a psychological block, which at times becomes a convenient "check" against reality. Her early marriage to Jacob Arnauti, a French national and an Albanian by descent, and the birth of a child who is subsequently kidnapped or lost are also vague as to timing.

Justine's first husband, Arnauti, enters the story only as author of a diary-novel, *Moeurs*, in which he colorfully exploits his marriage to Justine, therein called Claudia. This document is freely quoted from by Darley and is useful in filling in the psychological origins of Justine. Apparently Arnauti married and divorced Justine when they were both very young, and Arnauti was not necessarily the father of her child. The situation is not clearly defined. Soon the "lost child" becomes a theme which is woven into the story at several levels. Justine's search for the little girl motivates much of her strange behavior. Her marriage to Nessim is at one point explained as the result of her need for Nessim's money and influence in carrying on the search. But, in the end, one is uncertain about the child's fate—and about Justine's "real" attitude toward her lost child. The search, per se, seems a psychological necessity to Justine. Possibly she conceals her knowledge of certain facts in order to continue indefinitely the *appearance* of the search.

The other important events in Justine's life involve most of the major characters in the story. Her marriage to Nessim, her intense and ambiguous relationships with lovers and friends—such as Darley, Clea, Pursewarden, Balthazar, Toto, and other Alexandrians—are discussed below in context. Justine is the most enigmatic character in the *Quartet*. Perhaps she is finally to be interpreted almost as one reads a Rorschach inkblot. She is each reader's unique projection of the fatal woman.

Darley's involvement with Justine begins casually when she attends a lecture of his on the Alexandrian poet, Cavafy, and takes him home after the lecture to meet her handsome, wealthy husband. And, throughout his affair with Justine, Darley remains friends, at varying degrees of intensity and complexity, with Nessim Hosnani. Justine's husband's cuckoldry seems both fantastic and calculated. Immensely wealthy and dashingly sophisticated, Nessim is intelligent and wary. Educated in Germany and in England, he combines the older Egyptian traditions with the modern "know-how." He is a Copt—a proud yet exotic Christian. The layers of intrigue and ambiguity that make up his personality unfold as the story unfolds, and his inscrutable nature is exposed as a function of mysticism and shrewdness. He is involved politically and psychologically with such unlike characters as Cohen, Melissa, Pursewarden, and Mountolive. But, by the end of the fourth volume, Nessim has lost most of his nimbus of mystery; and his behavior seems almost pedestrian. His Faustian tendencies are revealed as something less than exalted.

In the beginning of the story, both Justine and Nessim Hosnani are highly glamorous figures to Darley. They move easily in decadent and lavish pre-war Alexandria. Justine's compliance as Darley's mistress becomes the climax of his comparatively uneventful life, and Darley remembers this quasi-religious event with awe and gratitude. It endows all of Alexandria with radiance. As Darley gradually elaborates his relationships with Justine and her friends, a truly fabulous "City" emerges.

Alexandria is a major character in the story. Again and again Darley explicates and describes it and its interesting inhabitants. He tells of Mnemjian's barber shop, a favorite haunt of the Alexandrians. Mnemjian is himself one of the most colorful of the denizens of Alexandria—"a dwarf with a violet eye that has never lost its childhood" (J:36). He is both barber and procurer, and later serves as a messenger. Allegedly a member of an espionage grapevine, Mnemjian is central to the dissemination of Alexandrian gossip. His customers make up a kind of club in which the members play significant roles in the narrative patterns of the *Quartet*. At the shop such Alexandrians as Capodistria, Pombal,

Toto, Scobie, Keats, and Balthazar meet to exchange news and to be informed. Each of these characters eventually enters decisively into one or more aspects of the story and needs to be identified at this point in the summary of the *Quartet* in order to clarify later events.

Paul Capodistria, described as "more of a goblin than a man" (*J*:33), is nicknamed the "Great Porn" and "Da Capo" (for *great pornographer* and *back to the beginning again*) as a tribute to his legendary sexual prowess. Supposed to be very rich, Capodistria is descended from a family of suicides and neurotics. His role is shaded in mystery. He is later identified as Justine's seducer. A member of the esoteric "Cabal," he is adept at black magic; he is certainly a Mephistophelean type, elusive and unveracious, subject to many shifts and changes. Even his death is faked at the end of *Justine*.

George Gaston Pombal, a minor French consular official, shares a flat with Darley in *Justine*. A great dispenser of advice, he browses through the story, busying himself with love affairs—his own and others. He introduces Darley to Arnauti's book about Justine. At that time he has just cast off his current mistress, the little model Sveva. Described as "a pegamoid sloth of a man" (*J*: 21), Pombal is involved in the espionage net covering pre-war Alexandria. He is most memorable finally for his fun-loving nature. His excursions into slapstick contrast with his romantic-tragic love affair with Fosca, his *respectable* mistress. Pombal is a well-rounded character toward whom the novelist never condescends.

Toto de Brunel, one of the many psychosexual deviates in Durrell's Alexandria, makes his major contribution to the story in the second volume where his brief and fragile life is sacrificed to plot exigencies when he is stabbed with a hatpin. His murder is followed by the usual equivocal explanations. Toto, although more fully drawn than most, is typical of the many eccentric Alexandrians who flit in and out of the balls and carnivals. He is a lightweight, appropriately sketched in pastels.

Joshua Scobie, another colorful Alexandrian deviate, is clearly defined. An aged Bimbashi in the Egyptian police, Scobie is literally transformed into a saint and legend within the covers of the *Quartet*. During the tense pre-war days, he is promoted to the secret police. There his "tendencies" and his ingenuousness as a policeman combine in a comedy of errors that ends in his tragic and disgraceful death while he is dressed as a tart. After his death a series of amusing coincidences elevates his old bathtub, in which he used to make home-brew, to a sacred relic; and the memory of him in his neighborhood is merged with the memory of a nearly forgotten saint so that the shrine of "El Yacoub" becomes Scobie's shrine and Scobie becomes a saint! Many of the most amusing anecdotes in the *Quartet* have to do with Scobie; with his green parrot of the scandalous vocabulary; and with his extraordinary friends, Toby, Budgie, Abdul, and others.[2]

Although Scobie's apotheosis occurs after death, the transformation of John Keats, the blue-eyed Global Agency correspondent in Alexandria, takes place within his own lifetime. Keats first enters the story in *Justine* as a restless, inquiring reporter with a camera. Insecure and easily upset, Keats tries earnestly to understand the strange doings of the Alexandrians. In the last volume he appears strong, handsome, and much matured by his war experiences and the proximity of death. Darley notes his resemblance to a Greek god. Keats's ultimate fate is hazy, however. At one time he expresses a premonition that he will marry Clea, but the novelist seems to leave his love-life unresolved. Darley predicts in the second volume that Keats "is to be killed in the desert, in full possession of his imbecility" (*B*:26). In the last volume Darley bids Keats a rather general "Vale" (*C*:187).

The most colorful of the Alexandrians who meet in Mnemjian's barber shop is the physician, S. Balthazar. Balthazar gives his name to the second volume, which he co-authors; but he is seen frequently in all four volumes. He is described by Darley as "one of the keys to the City." Darley adds: "If Mnemjian is the archives of the City, Balthazar is its Platonic *daimon*—the mediator between its Gods and its men" (*J*:91). Tall, thin, and stooped, Balthazar usually wears a black hat with a narrow brim. Homosexual and "hermetic," he is much given to insights and aphorisms. A kind of prophet, he calls himself the "Wandering Jew": and, indeed, he seems eternal and ubiquitous. He knows all the major characters in the story. Darley's friend, Clea Montis, paints pictures for his records of his patients' lesions and operations. He is intimate with the Hosnanis and their circle. Balthazar's role as physician gives him access to everyone's secrets and symptoms. Also, as a member of the "Cabal," he decodes and solves mysteries.

In the first volume Darley has not the benefit of Balthazar's knowledge about Alexandria and the Alexandrians, but in the second volume Balthazar's corrections and emendations of the "facts" as recorded by Darley in the first volume become exciting new insights. In the first volume Darley still believes that Justine loves him deeply and that their affair is progressing predictably—jealous husband and all. Although he conjectures that Nessim may be having Justine watched, Darley remains friends with the husband of his mistress. One night Nessim and Darley, searching together for Justine, find her in a house of child prostitutes, seemingly in a state of shock. They take her home. The assumption is that Justine has been hunting for her lost child.

When the novelist, Pursewarden, moves in with Darley and Pombal for a time, Darley and Pursewarden become close friends; and another strand is added to the complicated patterns of Darley's life, one which he will never succeed in unravelling completely. Ludwig Pursewarden enters the lives of most of the Alexandrians at several levels and at several different entrances; and even his exit, as a suicide, is equivocal and enigmatic. Darley comes to know Pursewarden as a conversationalist, poet, and novelist. In the latter capacity he is author of a trilogy called *God is a Humorist*. Justine displays works by him in her bedroom. At first Pursewarden gives Darley "the impression of a young man lying becalmed in his mother" (*J*:54). But he is perceived by his associates variously, although usually as puzzle and enigma. His cultivated ironic tone baffles and irritates duller souls. Like one of his own characters, he may be identified as a member of "that ancient secret society—the Jokers" (*J*:201). And one of his best jokes may be his suicide, including a legacy to Darley of five hundred pounds to be spent on Melissa! Various "explanations" of the suicide are offered as the story progresses, and, paradoxically, Pursewarden's significance in the story increases after his death. He must be reckoned with in all four volumes—alive or dead.

The first volume of the *Quartet* in some ways is only the overture to the big novel. It introduces the major characters and situations, sketches in the backdrops, and indicates the basic patterns (although the surfaces will change) in the relationships which interlock the characters and the "City" in the multi-dimensional universe set up by Durrell. In this universe Justine, who gives her name to the first volume, persists to the end of the tetralogy—and even beyond.[3] And Clea, who gives her name to the fourth volume, begins to emerge in the first. In the beginning Darley's awareness of Clea Montis (her last name seems to relate her to Venus, although it is not used very often in the story) is tangential and casual. She remains on the periphery of Darley's experience, for this is her seed-time. Clea's harvest-time comes in the fourth volume, and in the end her transformation from insecurity to maturity is the clearest story-line in the *Quartet.*

Like other major characters, Clea is both participant and observer; and she observes with the professionally trained eye of the artist. In addition to the clinical paintings she does for Balthazar, she works on portraits of Scobie and Justine (both apparently never finished). She paints a portrait of Mountolive as ambassador to Egypt—in full-dress uniform. She does a chalk drawing of Nessim, prints Pursewarden's death mask, and designs a nose for Dr. Amaril's beloved, the virtuous Semira, who was born noseless. Later Clea experiments with abstract painting.

The Clea of the first three volumes is superstitious, believes in "scrying" and following hunches. She is addicted to horoscopes and believes in charms against evil. Later she gains more assurance as she puts away her childish dependencies. She is always eclectic in her personal relationships. In addition to her final and deep attachment to Darley, she is, in passing, Scobie's good friend, Justine's short-term lover, Melissa's patron saint, Narouz' secret love object, and Dr. Amaril's mistress. Done in tones of honey-gold and blue—gold hair and blue eyes—Clea's lighted beauty contrasts with Justine's shadowed seductiveness.

The vignettes and fragmentary backflashes that make up Darley's narrative in the first volume are surprisingly informative despite the seeming lack of coherence. Although the first impression of the narrative technique suggests confusion, the confusion is planned. Facts emerge and patterns of facts are clearly discernible as rewards for careful reading. As the past is transformed into the present, time passes once again in Darley's memory. Melissa is ill. Darley attends Cohen's deathbed and receives from him the rings which Cohen bought for Melissa but never gave to her. (These are the rings which Darley has buried under the hearthstone—referred to at the very beginning of the volume.) Pursewarden commits suicide. Then Darley retraces the degrees of intensification marking his affair with Justine, an improbable affair made all the more exciting by its improbability. Time is often confounded in these backflashes, but one significant season is focused by Darley—the second spring of the love affair. Justine and Darley have grown increasingly apprehensive, for a series of incidents indicates that Nessim is having them watched and may be preparing a dramatic retaliation.

At this time all Alexandria is restless and unsafe, for war threatens. Some comedy relief is momentarily afforded by Scobie's bungling attempts, as new head of the secret police, to apprehend suspects, including many Alexandrians—in general the wrong ones! When Darley helps Scobie—mainly as a lark—he finds the name of Cohen on the suspect-list. Meanwhile, Nessim is having a "Summer Palace" built in the desert for Justine. There he installs a holy man as caretaker. Loyal (or perfidious, for who can be sure?) servants do strange and ambiguous things. Omens, warnings, threats continue to surround the lovers, Justine and Darley. When Balthazar loses the small key which he uses to wind his watch, the key is returned by Nessim to Justine, from whom Nessim has apparently stolen it. And Nessim begins to have a series of spectacular dreams. On the edge of a nervous breakdown, he starts to entertain lavishly, hysterically. The king is a frequent guest at the great Hosnani house. Alexandria talks much of the Hosnani wealth and hospitality.

In an introspective mood, Darley searches for the meaning of it all. He dons a tarbush and goes into the native Quarter where he observes a mating in a whorehouse (the male component is later identified as Mnemjian or Narouz). The awkwardness and the grossness of the act which Darley observes make him ponder on sex and love. His attempt to objectify the subjective is anguished and desperate. A climax in the psychological as well as the physical aspects of the story is approaching.

As the time for Nessim's annual duck shoot—a pretentious event—draws near, Justine expresses her fear that Darley may be murdered at the shoot. Nessim, apparently deeply troubled, turns to Melissa for comfort; and from this "comfort" Melissa's child, the girl Darley has with him on the island, is eventually born. But, despite the premonition of disaster, Darley is not killed at the duck shoot—not even shot at. The victim of an ill-aimed or maliciously well-aimed shot is Capodistria, now identified as Justine's seducer, the man wearing the black patch. Capodistria's death seems convenient, for now Justine may be freed from her psychological block. Later events, however, show that the affair was rather prosaically political rather than erotic. Capodistria's death is revealed in the sequel as faked. Another body, an unidentified corpse, was substituted for Capodistria's.

At the end of the first volume, however, many puzzles are still unsolved—deliberately so in most situations. Darley believes "Da Capo" is dead. After the duck shoot Justine abruptly leaves for Palestine. Clea eventually sees her there and reports in a letter to Darley that the de-glamorized Justine is working on a farm. Darley then says farewell to Melissa, for he is going to teach school in Upper Egypt. (He will return to Alexandria apparently only once in two years, when Melissa dies.) Darley spends his last night in Alexandria with Clea—but without making love to her! Thus the first telling of this thrice-told tale concludes quietly. All passion is spent—for the time being.

II Balthazar

Balthazar, the second volume of the *Quartet*, covers approximately the same time span as the first volume, but it wears its rue with a difference. Between the end of *Justine* and the opening of *Balthazar*, Darley gave his manuscript—the story as told in *Justine*, to Balthazar to read. Now Balthazar comes in person to the small Mediterranean island where Darley, with Melissa's young daughter, has lived "two or three winters" (*B*:16). Balthazar leaves with Darley the original manuscript with his own comments and emendations. Darley then proceeds to retell his story, revising, adding, and quoting extensively from Balthazar's corrections and notes, the substance of which is referred to as the "Great Interlinear."

Darley recalls the group which used to meet in Mnemjian's barber shop: Capodistria, Pombal, Keats, Scobie, and Toto. Again the past is turned into the present as Darley reconstructs once more the pre-war Alexandrian scene. With the help of Balthazar's gossipy notes, he reflects on Justine and Clea. And a new name appears among the Alexandrians: David Mountolive, English ambassador to Egypt, for whom Nessim has given a party.

Mountolive is the interesting and complex character who gives his name to the third volume of the *Quartet*. His "story" begins to emerge in *Balthazar,* dominates the third volume, and is not quite completed by the end of the *Quartet*. Mountolive first came to Alexandria as a junior in the state department. As a very young man he was befriended by the Hosnanis and became for a short time the lover of Leila Hosnani, the mother of Nessim and Narouz. This romance is described in detail in the third volume. In the second volume Mountolive has returned to Alexandria as ambassador after a lapse of some years. He is seen as the party-giving and party-going Sir David, popular, handsome, and very British. His former mistress, now a veiled recluse, her face disfigured by smallpox, is nervously aware of his presence—for personal and political reasons.

Of course, Darley at first knows nothing of these complications. As he studies Balthazar's notes, he gets new insights—some of them startlingly opposed to his first impressions—into the lives and loves of his friends. Balthazar, for example, reveals the cool and seemingly secure Clea as emotionally dependent upon her father. And Clea's abnormal love for Justine is analyzed as a transient, fragile thing. Becoming more and more curious—and disturbed— Darley ponders on the various kinds of sexuality involved in love. The story patterns now begin to reveal new textures and more facets.

Darley reconstructs a complicated version of Nessim's courtship of Justine, and he also re-evaluates the whole Hosnani family, noting now the relative importance of Nessim's brother, Narouz. Nessim's "love" for Justine has included (or has been based upon) her Jewish background as an asset in the political conspiracy against English interests in Egypt which Nessim and his brother are leading for profit and pleasure. Nessim, as a Copt, detests the English. He has sympathized with Palestine during the local tensions.

Nessim's younger brother, Narouz, of no importance in the first volume, lives and dies primarily in the second and third volumes.

A blue-eyed, harelipped visionary, strong and passionate by nature, Narouz lacks his brother's measure and control. He is a killer and his potential for violence touches both Justine and Clea. His life is short and intense, for he himself is murdered at the end of the third volume; but, like the dead Pursewarden and the dead Scobie, he lives on in the memories of the others—and is effective even from beyond the grave. Narouz' harpoon gun, carelessly handled by Balthazar, is the instrument which later wounds Clea *after* Narouz' death.

Leila Hosnani, vital mother of the Hosnani brothers, was one of the first Coptic women to give up the veil and to interest herself in the "world of scope." However, she abandoned most of her worldly interests after her marriage to Falthaus Hosnani, who appears in the third volume as an ill-tempered invalid. According to Balthazar, Leila has blessed the marriage of Nessim and Justine, but not without innuendos of possible violence against Justine should she not be a good wife. Justine renounces Judaism and becomes a Copt, and the wedding is solemnized at the Hosnani estate, Karm Abu Girg.

The most unpredictable revelation to come from Balthazar's emendations and corrections is the claim that Justine has used Darley as a decoy, that her real love has been Pursewarden all along. Pursewarden's legacy to Darley is thus seen as payment for Pursewarden's use of Melissa as *his* decoy and for Justine's use of Darley as *her* decoy. And, apparently, both Darley and Pursewarden were decoys in Nessim's political conspiracy.

In the process of these revelations, Pursewarden is more fully characterized. In the second volume Pursewarden appears most often as ironist. He is much quoted on many subjects, and his ideas no doubt reflect those of Henry Miller, Wyndham Lewis, D. H. Lawrence (whom Pursewarden has known personally), and, of course, Durrell himself. The "uses" of Pursewarden and his many views on love, art, and God are discussed in the following two chapters of this study. His "Obiter Dicta," printed in the "Consequential Data" appended to the second volume of the *Quartet,* are quasi-scriptural and are useful in explicating the theory which motivates all this mystification.

Pursewarden's erotic techniques with Justine are coarse but effective. Pursewarden's capacity for love and sex is large, and his versatility is attested to in later volumes. His sister, Liza, and Darley's mistress, Melissa, must be added to the list of his bedmates—in addition to his current mistress, Justine; a wife back home; and the casual contacts of a healthy man in a wicked city. There were many reasons for Pursewarden to live; few reasons for him to die. Yet death needs only one reason—and often a trivial one.

Justine's despair at Pursewarden's sudden suicide is described by Balthazar and retold by Darley. Further details of this ambiguous event are now revealed, such as a fragment of an inscription left by Pursewarden on his bathroom mirror just before he killed himself. The mystery thickens. Meanwhile another of the mysteries, the disappearance of Justine's child, is of persistent concern to Nessim in the second volume. Nessim enlists the aid of his brother to recover the child or at least to learn of her fate. At the feast of *Sitna Mariam* Narouz seeks knowledge of the lost child from the Magzub, a religious known as the "Inspired One." At one time the Magzub himself has been suspected of kidnapping the child. Now he shows Narouz a vision of the death of the child by drowning. Details seen by Narouz in the vision, such as clothing and jewelry, check out correctly. But Nessim, informed by Narouz of the child's fate, does not tell Justine, who has become increasingly anxious. She finally confesses that she borrowed Balthazar's watch key in order to try to open Nessim's wall safe in the hope of finding papers about her lost child after she partially overheard a telephone conversation between Nessim and Narouz about the Magzub incident.

The tension increases as Darley continues to reconstruct the past. About this time Scobie dies, violently and comically; he is "done in" by some sailors while he is "cruising" the docks dressed as a tart. And Pombal's affair with his current mistress, Sveva, also ends in comic violence as she smashes his car. Pombal can now move on to the great affair of his life, his affair with Fosca, which will end tragically in *Clea*.

Balthazar's notes suggest that Nessim may be trying to do away with Justine; but she continues to use Darley as distraction and as informant. The scene is now set for violence, in this second version of the story, just as it was in the first volume before the duck shoot. This time the violence comes at the Cervonis' carnival ball. Toto de Brunel is murdered, and several explanations are advanced. Toto was a secret agent and was removed for political reasons. Toto, disguised in a domino and wearing Justine's ring at her request, was killed by Nessim's agent who thought he was Justine. The "real truth" comes out when Clea tells Balthazar that Narouz has confessed the killing to her; Narouz thought he had stabbed Justine for making a pass at him. Of course Toto had made the pass at Narouz in his own name, so to speak, while wearing Justine's ring. For Toto, the tragedy of errors is finished. For Narouz, too, a resolution in his life is approaching. He asserts his love for Clea to Clea, who finds this unsolicited affection disgusting and unfair. Narouz, rejected, turns in upon himself and stands now at the edge of madness.

The second volume closes with a letter from Clea, who is in Syria, about two years after the events retold by Darley with Balthazar's help. Clea encloses a letter from Pursewarden (he is "now" dead), and she refers to many of their mutual friends. She believes that her old friend, Scobie, died from an innocent fall down the stairs. Truth wears many faces. Clea also believes that she and most of the others will return some day to Alexandria. The second volume closes quietly, too; for the same passion as in the first volume has been spent—albeit somewhat differently!

III Mountolive

In the third volume of the *Quartet* Darley bows out as narrator. The story is largely told by the omniscient novelist. Several new characters appear, and more than several new facts are revealed about the old characters. The story of the third volume begins with the coming of the young David Mountolive to Egypt—a projection farther back into the past than the time of the first two volumes. Mountolive, attractive and eager, is sent to Egypt early in his diplomatic career to improve his Arabic. When he is befriended by the Hosnanis, he is pleased; for he wants to learn as much as possible about exotic Egypt. He rides and hunts with the brothers; makes love to the mother, Leila; and argues with the father, Falthaus, a cadaverous invalid. Older than his beautiful wife, Falthaus is a Coptic squire living in the feudal tradition, and ardently anti-British. Young Mountolive, in love with Falthaus' wife, finds Falthaus hostile but intelligent. Several years after the affair between Leila and Mountolive, Falthaus dies; but he leaves his mark on his sons, who are equally intense, each in his own way.

The love of the mature but passionate Leila Hosnani is a first and deep experience for the young Mountolive. Leila teaches him what his English education has neglected: "The social man in him was overripe before the inner man had grown up" (*M:18*). Their ten days' intimacy changes him from boy to man, and Leila's influence extends far beyond the brief bedroom interlude. After smallpox takes her beauty from her, Leila solaces herself with a lengthy and profound correspondence with her former boy-lover, now becoming increasingly important in the world of diplomacy. Leila's role in his life as confidante and correspondent further refines Mountolive's sensibilities. For years he continues to write to her everything about himself, including accounts of later affairs with other women.

After leaving Egypt the young Mountolive is posted to the mission in Prague, then to Oslo, Berne, Japan, Lima, Portugal, Helsinki, and finally Russia—wherever he has no use for the Arabic that he so conscientiously had learned. Once, while in England, he looks up Pursewarden at Leila's request; Leila has been interested in Pursewarden's poetry. At that time he also meets Pursewarden's blind sister, Liza, who rather unexpectedly becomes an important new character in the story. Liza Pursewarden is strikingly beautiful, with "the marble whiteness of the sea-goddess' face . . ." (*M:162*). Her life-story, which emerges more fully in the last two volumes, includes an incestuous love affair with her brother and a marriage to Mountolive.

Mountolive does not yet foresee his involvement with Liza, but he finds her attractive and interesting. When he learns later in Russia that he is to become Sir David, ambassador to Egypt, he is both hopeful and fearful. He buys his chief's dress uniform, has it altered to fit his own slimness, and returns to England—this time by way of Berlin. In Berlin he visits briefly with Nessim, who is dining with international munitions kings. In England he stays with his mother at Dewford Mallows, and the implications of a close mother-son relationship and references to the existence of an absent, scholarly father, who is mainly memorable for the gift of a Tibetan prayer wheel to his young son, round out Mountolive's background.

In some ways Mountolive embodies the "English death" drama-
tized in *The Black Book*. Perceptive and introspective, he learns
gradually but thoroughly that his power as ambassador is limited
and that his integrity as a man is often equivocal. He becomes
increasingly disillusioned as his story unfolds; and, although he
continues to appear as the handsome Englishman who sits resplendent in his dress uniform as Clea paints his portrait, he is
disturbed by rumors of his friends' betrayals of trust. Pursewarden's suicide and Nessim's treason eventually become major
concerns to him.

Before leaving for Egypt, Mountolive confers in London with
his colleague, Kenilworth, who cautions him against retaining
Pursewarden in his post in Alexandria. It appears that Pursewarden, a minor official, has alienated Maskelyne, chief of the war
office, because Maskelyne has suspected the Hosnanis of conspir-
ing against British interests. Pursewarden denies the possibility.
Furthermore, he has asked Mountolive in a letter not to counter-
mand a transfer out of Egypt which Pursewarden has asked for.
In his letter Pursewarden describes official embassy life sardoni-
cally and fills in on Justine's love life. He tells Mountolive how
Justine and Darley were almost apprehended *flagrante delicto*
by Maskelyne, and he goes on to defend Nessim against Maskelyne's charges.

Despite some uneasiness, Mountolive decides to get Maskelyne
instead of Pursewarden transferred out of Egypt. He promotes
Pursewarden. Mountolive is welcomed to Cairo by all members of
his staff except Pursewarden, who is said to be indisposed. Soon,
as is customary in summer, the whole office moves to Alexandria.
There Mountolive renews friendships with Balthazar, Amaril,
Clea, Nessim, and Justine. Although Leila remains inaccessible,
Mountolive has much to keep him busy. All in all, he enjoys his
first summer in Alexandria as the new ambassador; and in the
autumn he moves back to Cairo—without seeing Leila. At carnival time, despite her promise, she does not meet him. Mountolive
glimpses Amaril and Amaril's mysterious new mistress, a noseless
girl, Semira, whose story is then told to Mountolive by Clea as she
paints his portrait.

Clea tells him how Dr. Amaril found his "perfect woman" in the
masked Semira during a carnival, when Amaril and Semira made

love without unmasking. Only later does Amaril discover that Semira has no nose. Semira is the rather simple-minded daughter of a very old and deaf father, who agrees to her marrying Amaril. In the sequel, Clea designs her a nose, and Amaril constructs it. Then Semira is trained by Amaril to become a doll's surgeon while Clea coaches her in the ways of the world. Thus, in a real sense, Semira becomes the joint creation of Clea and Amaril.

While Mountolive learns more and more about his old friends in Alexandria, the troubled Pursewarden has a critical experience. On a ramble about town he meets Melissa, with whom he spends the night. From her he learns that Nessim is definitely plotting against British interests and realizes that he was wrong in denouncing Maskelyne's charges against Nessim. Meanwhile, Pursewarden has received five hundred pounds from Leila for composing an epitaph for her uncle. He makes a will leaving the money to Darley, and then he kills himself by swallowing a cyanide tablet. He leaves a sealed letter for Mountolive informing him of the Hosnani treachery and of his own delinquency in the case. He also leaves a message written with a shaving stick on his mirror: "NESSIM. COHEN PALESTINE ETC. ALL DISCOVERED AND REPORTED" (*M*:215). The first on the scene after Pursewarden's suicide, Nessim erases most of the message before being interrupted. Now both Mountolive and Nessim must act more directly and certainly sooner than they had intended—and on opposite sides.

In a backflash the reader learns that Nessim's attractiveness to Justine has involved his political ambitions more than his person. Justine is spying on *both* Darley and Pursewarden. Conspiracy and the fear of death are aphrodisiacs to her. Nessim and Justine plan and execute the elaborate maneuvers which include Justine's affairs with Darley and Pursewarden and the lavish entertainments and other red herrings necessary to their plot. One night Justine reports to Nessim that they need not fear Melissa, for Darley's prostitute-mistress knows nothing. This assumption, of course, is the fatal mistake. Melissa is the one who informs Pursewarden of Nessim's treachery. Cohen had told her!

Back at Karm Abu Girg, Leila Hosnani has been alarmed at the extent of the conspiracy. She learns that in six months the objectives will be accomplished. Then both Justine and Leila are to go away. Since Capodistria's part in the plot has been compromised, "Da Capo" is to be *apparently* killed at the great duck shoot. Narouz, however, remains a problem; for his fanaticism is so endangering the measured progress of their plans that Nessim thinks he may have to do away with his brother. When he cautions Narouz against impetuousness, Narouz is surly and rude. He accuses Nessim of having sold their mother some years before to the "British swine," Mountolive.

Pursewarden's suicide, which comes at this critical time, is variously interpreted. Balthazar sees it as a gesture of contempt for the world. Mountolive, after reading Pursewarden's confession letter, attributes it to Pursewarden's delinquency in the Hosnani case. And at least one more "explanation" awaits the revelations of Pursewarden's sister, Liza. When substantiating proof of Pursewarden's delinquency comes to Mountolive in a letter from Maskelyne, Mountolive decides to take immediate action against Nessim. He notifies the Egyptian authorities.

Nessim seems relieved that the issue has been defined. His recently observed pistol practice and research in poisons had nothing to do with husbandly jealousy but were motivated by his concern for his personal safety. Now he goes into more subtle action. He bribes the minister of the interior, the corrupt and infinitely corruptible Memlik Pasha, to delay intervention in the case by presenting him with copies of the Koran (Memlik is a collector) richly interleaved with money. The bribes assure Nessim time to perfect his coup for Palestine against Egyptian interests.

Mountolive finally sees Leila again when she decides to plead with him on behalf of her sons. The interview, in a carriage at night, between the troubled diplomat and the veiled, rather smelly old lady whom Mountolive simply does not recognize as the once-beautiful love of his youth, is far from romantic. Mountolive dismisses Leila, and in revulsion goes off disguised as a native into an adventure which ends in a child brothel to which he is mistakenly sent by a casual acquaintance. Later that night, Mountolive returns to the embassy, chastened and feeling increasingly inadequate.

Memlik, pressured by Mountolive and realizing that he must ultimately take at least some token action in the name of Egypt's welfare against the Hosnani conspiracy, is advised by his toady,

Rafael, to move against the relatively harmless Narouz instead of against Nessim. Narouz, alone at Karm Abu Girg, is murdered by Memlik's agents. The death of Narouz, which concludes this third version of the doings of the Alexandrians, is dramatic and protracted. Although the dying man's desire to see Clea is not granted, Balthazar is with him at the end. And the Coptic wake which follows Narouz' death is an appropriate tribute to the visionary, tragic figure who has become a sacrificial victim to Alexandrian intrigue.

IV Clea

The fourth volume of the tetralogy differs from the other three in that it projects the story on in time. Most of the action of *Clea* occurs after the events previously recorded. In this last volume Darley resumes as narrator. He is preparing to return to Alexandria from his "island retreat." The time is the last year of the war, but of course Darley does not know it is the *last* year. Mnemjian, now the richest barber in war-prosperous Egypt, comes to the island as a messenger from Nessim. He informs Darley that Darley's return to Alexandria would be convenient now for all concerned. He gossips about the Alexandrians: Balthazar has been ill; the Hosnani conspiracy has collapsed; Nessim and Justine are poor; Justine is under house arrest at Karm Abu Girg. Nessim, who works as an ambulance driver, has lost an eye and a finger. Pombal, now high man with the Free French, confers often these days with Mountolive. Capodistria is alive!

Darley has decided to take with him back to Alexandria Melissa's child by Nessim. This little girl, who was referred to in the first volume by the name of "Justine" (*J*:118), is a rather shadowy figure. Darley was informed by Balthazar after Melissa's death that the child was at Nessim's summer palace and that Nessim wished to give her up. Darley agreed to care for her. Now, on the island, he has prepared her for her eventual return to Nessim by teaching her to think of her "parents" (Nessim and Justine) as "playing-card characters." The child has been adjusting to a fantasy invented for her by Darley, but one which is closer to the reality she can apprehend than the simple truth would be.

Upon Darley's return to Alexandria with the child, Nessim meets them at the landing, and Darley gives the child to her father; and Darley sees that the war has marked the "City." In some ways it is more beautiful than ever. With awe and horror, he describes the colorful spectacle of the bombing of the harbor.

At the request of Mountolive, Darley is given a job in "censorship." Darley then goes back to the flat he once shared with Pombal and Pursewarden. There poignant memories of Melissa greet him. His *recherche du temps perdu* includes meetings with his old friends, Pombal, Justine, Balthazar, and finally Clea.

Pombal has much to tell Darley. Pombal has fallen in love with a married woman; and, most extraordinary of all, he has not yet been to bed with her. His beloved, Fosca by name, has a husband, a British officer away in the war; and somehow passion has been checked by honor. Chastity is a new experience for Pombal. Pombal also gossips with Darley about Mountolive's love for Liza, the late Pursewarden's blind sister. Despite war, Alexandria still has its usual, high quota of sexuality.

Darley visits Karm Abu Girg, where a deteriorated Justine greets him. Her left eyelid droops as the result of a slight stroke. Melissa's child has adjusted to life in her new home, but Nessim and Justine are both tense and unhappy. Narouz' death has deeply disturbed Nessim, who has been blamed for it. Nessim is now driving an ambulance as part of his war service, and he seems eager to get away from his wife and home as much as possible. Justine explains to Darley that Nessim brought her back from Palestine. Now that Nessim is weak, she says, she feels no passion for him. Her feelings for Pursewarden, she insists, were incestuous and sick. She also laughs at Narouz' hopeless love for Clea as part of the madness of the past. But there is no conviction in her comments, and Darley knows that that part of his life is finished. Despite Justine's obvious reluctance to give him up, Darley leaves; he feels pity but no passion for his former mistress.

He visits the ailing and disgraced Balthazar, who has almost destroyed himself for the love of a worthless actor. Balthazar tells Darley that he is about to be "rehabilitated" by Clea and other friends who have not deserted him. Mountolive, at some trouble and expense, has arranged an elaborate public luncheon as a kind of coming-out party for the repentant physician. Balthazar explains to Darley how he provided a cadaver as a substitute for Capodistria at the duck shoot. Reverting to his role as adviser,

Balthazar recommends that Darley, who confesses that he has stopped writing, find Clea.

When Darley does see Clea, he realizes that she is more attractive to him than ever. As if life were neatly patterned, Darley finds Clea sitting where he had once found Melissa. Clea takes him to the shrine of El Yacoub where the late Scobie is now worshipped as "El Scob." She also takes him to the "Auberge Bleue," where Amaril's beloved Semira, now provided with a fine nose designed by Clea and executed by Amaril, is making her debut— just as Balthazar has made his new entrance into the world. The fourth volume is much concerned with rehabilitations like these, for time produces either death or redemption—or both. As Darley ponders these events and observes his old friends, he senses a new strength in Clea and feels a new love growing in himself. That night Clea and Darley become lovers.

Darley now begins to revise all his former impressions of Alexandria. A new kind of "reality"—quite opposed to carnival and war—is beginning to emerge for him. Clea tells him how much she has hated the carnival aspect of war-time Alexandria. She has been busy settling scores with her own past and searching out new, more stable meanings. She tells him that she once offered herself to Pursewarden to cure herself of her virginity and a "workblock" she thought was related to her virginity, but Pursewarden only laughed at her. Later, she confesses, she did find a satisfactory lover when she was in Syria, one who awakened her. When pregnant she had an abortion in order to remain free. She neither sentimentalizes nor understates her experiences. She seems increasingly objective and sane.

Clea also tells Darley what she knows about the growing love between Liza Pursewarden and Mountolive, and she tells him that she has purposefully delayed painting Liza's portrait. Liza has given Clea Pursewarden's notebooks, and Clea now passes them on to Darley to read; for they contain much about him as well as about other Alexandrians and, of course, about Pursewarden himself. And the "truth" about Pursewarden has never been simple. His notebooks reveal that he often pondered such controversial subjects as love, truth, art, poetry, sex, and literary theory. He recorded his conversations with Darley, whom he calls in his notes, not unaffectionately, "Brother Ass." He also narrates his version of the fate of Justine's lost child, explaining that Mnemjian had found the dead body of the little girl in a brothel and that Justine had seen the body just before Nessim and Darley came to drag her away—an episode recounted earlier (in the first volume) only from Darley's point of view.

After reading Pursewarden's notebooks, Darley visits Liza at the ambassador's summer residence, where she is staying as Mountolive's guest. Liza explains to Darley that she and her brother had been lovers and that she had had a child, a blind girl, who died. She fears that Keats, the reporter, is writing an unpleasant book about her brother at the request of her brother's wife. She explains Pursewarden's equivocal suicide as his self-sacrificing response to her love for Mountolive. Pursewarden, she believes, wanted to remove himself from the scene in order to free her. The death of their daughter had also depressed him. She goes on to explain to Darley that after her brother's death she decided to visit Alexandria and, in particular the British Embassy there and in Cairo, to gather materials for a book about Pursewarden. Now Mountolive has fallen in love with her and has proposed.

Darley talks with Keats, who dislikes Liza and sees her as a wily schemer. Keats also despises even the memory of the dead Pursewarden, so he has rejected the commission offered him by Pursewarden's widow to write a book about the novelist-poet-philosopher. Keats speaks his mind forcefully these days. Darley is much impressed by the change in him. He looks like a Greek god. In the exposure to death during the war, Keats has found "an inkling of Life Everlasting" (C:183).

Liza seems honest enough, however, to Darley. After reading—at Liza's request—Pursewarden's letters to his sister, Darley reluctantly helps Liza burn these marvelously poetic and literate items. Darley continues to ponder the enigma known as Pursewarden. He concludes that Pursewarden's "irony was really tenderness turned inside out like a glove" (C:176). The fantastically complicated Pursewarden may have been very simple after all. The mystery is a function of the observers, not of the observed. Keats's verdict is too harsh; Liza's, too self-centered.

A year passes, and the war begins to recede. Melissa's child thrives at Karm Abu Girg. Balthazar, also prospering again after his rehabilitation, takes Darley and Clea to Capodistria's "grave."

Of course "Da Capo" has long since left the country, and Clea, at the graveside of the unknown corpse substituted for Capodistria, reads aloud a letter from the "Great Porn" to Balthazar telling of his experiments in occultism. Capodistria has plunged into black magic. One of his experiments, in which ten homunculi are created, is adapted from Paracelsus. Capodistria has not lost his flair for imaginative unveraciousness. Or perhaps he *is* Mephistopheles! Scobie's prediction that Narouz would drag Clea down to the grave with him is revealed in the sequent conversation. The moment seems ominous.

A short time later, while Pombal and Fosca are sailing in the harbor, the now pregnant Fosca is killed by a bullet from a French warship which the lovers' insouciant handling of their small boat seemed to threaten.[4] And a decisive (and probably symbolic) accident also happens to Clea not long after. For one reason and another, Darley and Clea have been drifting apart. Darley decides to leave for an indefinite time. Just before his intended departure, on the "mulid of El Scob," Balthazar, Clea, and Darley sail in Clea's boat for one last holiday to the little island in the harbor which Narouz had always thought of as his own. There, while swimming underwater, Clea is struck by a harpoon from the dead Narouz' gun, which Balthazar has been carelessly handling. (Nessim had given his late brother's gun to Clea as a keepsake some time before.) Darley, who dives in to save Clea, finds that her hand has been pinned to the submerged wreck of a ship by the steel arrow shot from the harpoon gun and that she cannot free herself. By hacking at her hand with a knife, Darley frees her—then restores her to life with artificial respiration. Clea's hand is badly mutilated, however. At the hospital Clea is treated by Amaril, who is now revealed as her Syrian lover, the man who freed her from her psychological impasse. Darley is only mildly surprised at the revelation. He remarks: "Amaril was like a playing card which had always been there, lying before me on the table, face downwards. I had been aware of its existence but had never turned it over" (*C*:256).

At Clea's request, Darley goes alone that evening to the celebration of the anniversary of El Scob. There he learns from Balthazar that Justine is arranging a personal interview with Memlik in the hope of restoring the Hosnani fortune and status, and that

Leila, the "Dark Swallow," has died. Darley bids farewell to his long-time friend and informant, Balthazar; and the story ends—as far as a space-time novel ever ends—with an exchange of letters between Darley and Clea.

Darley, writing from his "little island," describes his simple life: "the picture of a man skimming flat stones upon the still water of the lagoon at evening, waiting for a letter out of silence" (*C:* 277). The letter from Clea arrives—addressed in an unfamiliar hand! But the news from Clea is good: "I have crossed the border and entered into the possession of my kingdom, thanks to the Hand" (*C:278*). Her new hand is made of steel, Clea explains; for Amaril was not able to restore her mutilated hand. Yet the new hand is better than the old; it paints true. Clea also reports the news of mutual friends. Justine has succeeded with Memlik: the Hosnanis are about to be rehabilitated.

Darley, at peace, starts to write the book that begins "Once upon a time . . ." (*C:282*). Now Darley and Clea will find happiness with one another. But, since this is a space-time novel, "Workpoints" appended to the fourth volume suggest several extensions of the narrative, such as "Hamid's story of Darley and Melissa"; the account of Justine's relationship to Memlik; an "encounter" between Balthazar and Arnauti in Venice; the troubled life of the child of the ballet dancer, Grishkin, and Mountolive; and something associated with Narouz called "the great battle of the sticks" (*C:283*). The story is infinitely expandable.[5]

CHAPTER 5

The Alexandria Quartet *as Experiment*

No, but seriously, if you wished to be—I do not say original but merely contemporary—you might try a four-card trick in the form of a novel; passing a common axis through four stories, say, and dedicating each to one of the four winds of heaven. A continuum, forsooth, embodying not a *temps retrouvé* but a *temps délivré*. The curvature of space itself would give you stereoscopic narrative, while human personality seen across a continuum would perhaps become prismatic? Who can say? I throw the idea out. I can imagine a form which, if satisfied, might raise in human terms the problems of causality or indeterminacy. . . . And nothing very *recherché* either. Just an ordinary Girl Meets Boy story. But tackled in this way you would not, like most of your contemporaries, be drowsily cutting along the dotted line! [1]

SPACE-TIME" is a scientific concept which is transmuted with some loss of accuracy into a poetic concept. Durrell's use of space-time and relativity theory in *The Alexandria Quartet* is perhaps only more or less serious, but the spectacular success of the work calls for explanation and evaluation of concept and theory. The *story* of the *Quartet*—with due reference to its complexity— has been summarized in the preceding chapter; but the *theory's* the thing wherein the novelist catches the conscience of the critic! The theory is elaborate, perhaps pretentious. Part scientific jargon and part metaphor, it explicates and confounds. But it can be grasped despite its protean surface. The key concepts are *time* and *space-time*. After they are "explained," the theory may be unlocked fairly easily.

I   *Time*

Insofar as a novel tells a story, the novelist is committed to dealing with time. The novelist may minimize the story line so that characterization dominates, or he may try to describe only what he sees reflected from the surfaces of reality; but, as soon as something happens in the novel, time passes; and as soon as time passes, something happens. Time is of the essence.

There are at least two kinds of time: first, what the clocks seem to deal with, the movement forward, generally called chronological time and thought of as *coming* and *going* in equal intervals. There seems to be sense in conceiving time as directional and irreversible, as moving steadily from past through present into the future. The second kind of time, often called psychological time, is an internalized awareness of sequences that do not usually correspond with the clock sequences. These internal sequences are thought of as distortions of outside reality, so that one hour may *seem* three hours when one is bored or a minute when one is happy. It would be just as logical to call the clock the distorter for failing to record psychological time properly. A clock really records no one's time except its own.

The novelist has *always* corrected time—not just since Sterne, Bergson, Proust, or Robbe-Grillet. A novelist is an adjuster of discrepancies, an easer of the tensions which arise between the two big kinds of time. The reader's memory of what happened on the first page combined with what is happening on the second page as he reads becomes a pattern in terms of traces in the reader—and nowhere else. The actual novel is a function of the reader *and* the text. Each text is uniquely experienced by each reader, and its *order* is psychological rather than chronological.

Durrell intercalates (his word) and interpenetrates his narrative in *The Alexandria Quartet* with an abundance of ways from a *here* which is never quite *here* to a *there* which is not a straight-line distance away from any particular *here*. Reasons for Pursewarden's suicide, for example, vary as a function of *place* and *time*. There are many Pursewarden-suicides. The *first* time is the first reference to the act, the *next* time is the second reference to the act, and so on. This kind of order is chronological in that it follows the order of the pages in the book. But at the end, when the reader sees the book as a whole, as if it had transparent leaves read in one flash of marvelous insight, there is really only one suicide—one act with many layers or facets.

II *Space-time*

Since space is curved, it follows that a straight line is not neces sarily the shortest path between two points and that Euclidian geometry is not necessarily the most efficient system for describing shapes and distances. Unless the variable *time* is added to the traditional three dimensions (the length of a line, the width or height of a plane, and the thickness of a solid), there's no way of completely describing reality. Time is the needed fourth dimension.

If two friends make an appointment to meet under the clock in the Hotel Biltmore and do not specify the *time*, their chances of meeting accidentally (the *probability* of that occurrence in a merely three dimensional universe) are decreased. Agreeing on a *time*, such as "four P.M.," increases their chances of meeting.

The hypothetical meeting of the two friends at the Hotel Biltmore will take place or not take place as a function of their respective knowledge of not only *where* the hotel is, but also *when* it is. The hotel itself is an event in space-time, fixed by four items of information—its location relative to Fifth Avenue and to Forty-Second Street, its height in the air, and the moment or moments of its existence as measured relative to the observed movements of another event like the position of the hands of a watch on a certain wrist. It would be impossible to meet there before the hotel was built and impossible after it has been razed. Some *time* in some specifiable *space* (or some *space* in some specifiable *time*), each relative to a given observer (or average of a group of observers such as earth-bound New Yorkers), fixes an event "known" to us in terms of the space-time of its existence.

I come from downtown, so I go uptown to the Biltmore. Another comes from uptown, so he goes downtown—and we have agreed long ago not to argue about who is right. We both are right, of course. We measure the location of the hotel along our own reference axes. For one it is ten blocks *south,* three blocks *east,* and one floor *up.* For me it is twenty blocks *north,* ten blocks *west,* and thirty floors *down.* (I arrive by helicopter!) Shifting the axes of reference will not change the *real* position of the hotel, but it will change my description of the event, and suggest the possibility that the total event known as the hotel, which includes the time specification, is certainly relative to me as observer. We do know, although we may not quite understand it, that there is no longer one universal time. There are only various times proper to various bodies in the universe, which will *seem* to agree for two bodies close together—as on the earth—but will never agree for bodies far apart.

A *continuum* is hostile to discreteness. It defies classification and anatomizings. It sticks together because it is continuous, not because its parts are sticky; for it has no parts. We live (and write) in a *space-time continuum.* The paradox that events in a space-time continuum may appear to be simultaneous (and the same in other respects), when *in reality* they never are, is a challenge to the writer. Since the reference axes are not fixed for events in the universe of behavior as they are for the east-westness or north-southness of the streets and avenues in New York City (on the map), it is possible to conceive of infinitely new dimensions in story-telling—and of sharper focuses and finer measurements.

Now that space, or objects and events *in* space, can not be measured without specifying the time variable, Euclid's system of describing objects and their relations to one another, although possibly esthetically satisfying, is uncomfortably parochial. Something *relatively* simple like the disappearance of the dependable straight line as an efficient way of getting from point to point has serious consequences. Order in the sense of *first, second,* and *third* —and in the sense of *before* and *after* or *inside* and *outside* and the other "signatures of time"—is not valid. In come the heraldic design, the continuum, and new metaphors such as revolving axes of reference to get new facts. Little paradoxes become profound truths; and mirror images, refracted light, paintings, photographs, verbal records such as diaries and letters, become as points of reference appropriate ways of describing and narrating. We are reminded that the story goes *forward* or *backward* relative only to the observer and that goals and starting lines to an observer halfway between are perceived only as force gradients. Goals repel or attract relative to other considerations. Starting lines can easily turn into goals, and goals into starting lines.

III   *The Theory*

An analysis of *The Alexandria Quartet* as an experiment in the space-time novel must deal with internal references to theory, for it is a self-conscious work. Near the beginning of *Justine* Darley recognizes that "only . . . in the silences of the painter or the writer can reality be reordered, reworked and made to show its significant side" (*J:*17). The reordering and the reworking in the *Quartet* begin at once.

The important concept of multiple mirrors which reflect the multiple dimensions of the newly perceived space-time is first introduced by Justine as she muses at her dressmaker's. She notices that her image is reflected in five different mirrors, and exclaims: "Look! five different pictures of the same subject. Now if I wrote I would try for a multi-dimensional effect in character, a sort of prism-sightedness. Why should not people show more than one profile at a time?" (*J:*27). Multi-dimensionality and prism-sightedness are the metaphors that suggest new techniques for telling the new truths about a universe without fixed points of reference. Darley's island—"this sunburnt headland in the Cyclades," where he is writing *Justine*—is an ideal observation post: "Surrounded by history on all sides, this empty island alone is free from every reference" (*J:*113).

Darley has been pondering Arnauti's assertion: "For the writer people as psychologies are finished. The contemporary psyche has exploded like a soap-bubble under the investigations of the mystagogues" (*J:*113). Storytellers who formerly spun yarns and created characters found that their measuring instruments were not reliable. The yarns and character analyses were only partial truths.

On the island and in relative isolation (the steamer comes only once a month), Darley feels free to recreate Alexandria and the people he remembers: ". . . to frame them in the heavy steel webs of metaphors which will last half as long as the city itself . . ." (*J:*114). Acknowledging the many-sidedness of the new concept of personality and the distortions of reality inherent in a universe which furnishes no *absolute* observation post, Darley is tentative: "I realize that each person can only claim one aspect of our character as part of his knowledge. To every one we turn a different face of the prism" (*J:*118-19).

From the "Consequential Data" appended to *Justine* a statement attributed to Pursewarden further refines the theory of the new novel. Pursewarden writes of the "n-dimensional novel trilogy":

"The narrative momentum forward is counter-sprung by references backwards in time, giving the impression of a book which is not travelling from a tomb but standing above time and turning slowly on its own axis to comprehend the whole pattern. Things do not all lead forward to other things: some lead backwards to things which have passed. A marriage of past and present with the flying multiplicity of the future racing towards one. Anyway, that was my idea" . . . [*sic*] (*J:*248).

Pursewarden's "n-dimensional novel" is not all new. In the traditional technique of *revisiting*, the traces of the first visit mingle with the immediate experience of the return visit so that the "momentum forward"—the revisit—is "counter-sprung" by references backwards in time. When these references backwards are identifiable as memories, when the narrator is "reliable" and tells you which is memory, which is happening now, and which is going to happen, the narrative technique is traditional.[2] But when *now* is *long ago* and also *yet to come*—in the sense that events usually perceived as sequential are perceived as simultaneous and events usually perceived as simultaneous are strung out in time—then chronological time is truly confounded with psychological time; and the narrative technique must adapt. The result is experimental in the sense of a try at the as yet untried.

In the "n-dimensional novel" there are no limits to the number of times the axes of reference may be rotated, so that at any moment and position in space-time an event may be described from any number of observation posts or measured from any number of reference points. There are an infinite number of "stories" in any "event," all functions of new orientations of the axes from which the locations of the characters are being measured. Tintern Abbey may be revisited infinitely.

The "Note" which introduces *Balthazar* is specific about the pattern and mode of the *Quartet*. The pattern is fourfold, the "soup-mix recipe of a continuum," three variables (called "sides" by Durrell) of space and one of time. The first three parts of the *Quartet* relate to space; the fourth, to time. Thus, the first three parts are "siblings" and not "sequels." Only the fourth part moves forward in time. The parts are also turned through "both subjective and objective modes." In *Mountolive,* for example, Darley becomes an object. In the other three volumes he is a subject.

There are, then, three space dimensions, one time dimension, and two modes. The problem is how to *use* the four space-time dimensions and the two modes (six variables in all) to effect the new result: "a morphological form one might appropriately call 'classical'—for our time" (*B:*"Note"). Pursewarden also rebels against the "absurd dictates of narrative form in prose" (*B:*117) —such as the *he saids, she saids,* the props of the trade—and he recommends increasing reader participation.

Psychologists measure stimulus patterns in degrees of structuredness. Insofar as the stimulus pattern perceived is relatively unstructured, the range of response (understanding) increases. Highly structured patterns leave little room for individual interpretations. Pursewarden's claim that the reader should rely more upon his own resources moves in the direction of the inkblot, the understructured stimulus pattern. It asks from the reader maximum projection. Subjective mode then takes over, and the reader creates the novel from the minimum materials provided. Blank pages in prose and silences in music are analagous, but so far most experimental writers have been content with wide margins, many dots, and short chapters here and there; and no composer has yet dealt in silences only!

To Pursewarden is ascribed "the idea of a series of novels with 'sliding panels.'" And Balthazar's "Interlinear" adds another "layer" to the original. Balthazar draws the analogy with "some medieval palimpsest where different sorts of truth are thrown down one upon the other, the one obliterating or perhaps supplementing another" (*B:*183). The idea of layers, sliding panels, revolving axes of reference, variable modes, and new, extended, or confounded dimensions in space-time—all suggest the impact of the theory of relativity as apprehended by a lay (nonmathematical) intelligence. Such intelligence perceives indeterminacy, infinity, star-time, and outerspace metaphorically. It projects instead of proving, and reflects mainly the emotive content of theory. It can become anxious. By the middle of *Balthazar* Darley asks, "How then am I to manipulate this mass of crystallized data in order to work out the meaning of it . . . ?" (*B*:183). Of course the scientist would manipulate the date mathematically, symbolically. Darley cries: "I wish I knew. I wish I knew" (*B*:184).

Another twentieth-century scientific concept involved in the relativity proposition deals with the indeterminate behavior of "quanta," and is essentially statistical. Of any minimum bit of matter its chances of doing this or that, of going here or there, is an event with a probability rating. Formerly scientists believed that the universe was lawful in a neat way, and that all predictions, to be scientifically accurate, had to come true—for sure. Now scientists are more sophisticated. They say that there is a certain chance that of three electrons, two will do this or that in a certain time—but they do not specify which two. Pursewarden claims that his prose belongs "to the poetic continuum . . . it is intended to give a stereoscopic effect to character. And events aren't in serial form but collect here and there like quanta, like real life" (*B*:245). Quanta fall randomly. Events, like quanta, are properly thought of as statistical concepts. The novelist merely records their behavior.

The novelist as narrator in *Mountolive*, speaking as writer of the object book in the no-person proper to the Naturalist tradition, refers to "gravitational forces which lie inherent in the time-spring of our acts, making them spread, ramify and distort themselves . . ." (*M*:214). The *novelist* must appear to tame these forces with metaphors or redirect them, although the characters may appear to succumb. In *Mountolive* all the characters feel "the portents gathering around them—the paradigms of powers unleashed which must fulfil themselves" (*M*:214). Probabilities define the extent of their freedom. In this inferno of quasi-determinism Nessim is confused, for "if he could no longer control events, it was necessary that he should take control of himself, his own nerves" (*M*:220). He uses sedatives, which "only exorcized the twitchings of the subconscious temporarily." Nessim is up against it; so Balthazar suggests that Nessim record his dreams.

Dreams lie somewhere near the heart of the mystery about reality. They are one face of the prism, one wall of the prison, one more look from a relatively *uncensored* observation post at self and others. Also dreams transcend time, distort time, deliver us from time. Nessim's faith in reason is faltering. His last resorts are dream-analysis *and* self-discipline. These resorts *describe* his breakdown along conflicting dimensions. Finally, he appears to fight even against the novelist who defines him; and, in so doing, he opens new story possibilities.

Theoretically, there are unlimited possibilities for exploiting the story material in the *Quartet* simply by "radiating out" in other directions—from *new* reference points in *old* directions or from *old* reference points in *new* directions, with all directions defined along four dimensions, three of space and one of time.[3] The "Workpoints" appended to *Clea* suggest other "stories" to be generated from the material. And significantly enough, the "Workpoints" are really part of the *Quartet*. The trailing off, after the last page of the story in *Clea,* with the page of "Workpoints" is artful. The *Quartet* never properly ends. There are no "endings" in curved space!

These particularities occur in the mood and voice of the novelist himself—they are the voices of Durrell as author. As for *Darley*-as-author—he is reported in *Clea* as feeling that he has failed; for the "intrusion of new knowledge" has continued to disrupt his "frame of reference" with "unforeseen, unpredictable patterns" (*C*:12).

But Darley's failure is noble, for it is closer to "truth" than success would be. Yet the truth-value of a statement that paradoxically asserts its own inadequacy to communicate truth further complicates the "facts" of the case. Darley as unreliable narrator must ultimately be relied on, despite his assertion of his unreliability. That very assertion gives his unreliability a higher validity. "Truth is what most contradicts itself in time" (*B*:23).

Returning to Alexandria in *Clea*—the volume that extends on in clock-time—Darley once more revises truth, but now he has little hope of fixing truth once and for all. His "mania for exactitude" is lessening. Life itself is fiction. And not very reliable fiction at that![4]

In the end the theory in the work must be returned to the work as an inseparable part of its structure and meaning. The self-consciousness of the *Quartet* is one of the means to its effects. Darley has failed to "reorder and rework reality." Reality defeats him as a writer, frees him as a man. That is the truth as *Durrell* tells it.

IV *Points of View*

The theory of the space-time novel calls for diverse points of view embodied in various narrators and observers. A *conventional* sequence of events can be narrated by one voice in one person moving ahead on a straight line. A space-time novel, however, calls for spirals; cycles; and, above all, variations on themes and patterns. The reader is made to curve back toward the point of origin, varying again and again the old patterns at new levels. There is no *simple* motion of forwards or backwards. Directionality is always relative to the observer, and there is no stability except momentarily. Always there are *more* directions to be explored.

The major narrators in the *Quartet* are Arnauti, Darley, Pursewarden, Balthazar, and of course the novelist himself. Arnauti has written a diary of Alexandrian life as seen by a foreigner. The diary, called *Moeurs*, bears most heavily on the psychological origins of Justine, formerly Arnauti's wife. It ultimately appears to be an unreliable source of information. *Moeurs* is first presented to Darley by Pombal about one-fourth of the way through *Justine*. Up to that time Darley has been telling the story himself in a series of sketches and vignettes. *Moeurs* is tentative. Really only notes for a novel, it refers frequently to a character called Claudia, identified by Darley as Justine. Arnauti "maintains . . . that real people can only exist in the imagination of an artist strong enough to contain them and give them form." Arnauti's *theory* calls for a book, when he writes his novel, with a short synopsis of the plot on the first page, thus setting the book free from the demands of articulating the story: "What follows would be drama freed from the burden of form. *I would set my own book free to dream*" (J:75).

Darley's quotations from Arnauti's descriptions of Justine-Claudia are useful to Durrell in giving Justine a past—before Darley. Justine's "check" and other psychological traits are described by Arnauti. Soon Justine is compounded of at least three versions: Darley's Justine, Arnauti's Justine, and Nessim's Justine. Later, Pombal's evaluation of a passage from *Moeurs* adds another dimension. And Nessim's agents prepare a dossier on Justine checking the validity of the other "versions." Pombal and the agents are, however, no more reliable than Arnauti.

Both Pursewarden and Clea eventually "repudiate Arnauti." Nevertheless, Arnauti's book is very useful to the novelist. Of Justine Darley notes: "The pages of Arnauti run through my mind as I watch her and talk to her" (*J*:136). Darley quotes Arnauti to himself, debates Arnauti's observations on Justine while he himself is lying beside Justine, so that two Justines, Arnauti's and Darley's, form a counterpoint with a third Justine, the one lying there—not one the *real* Justine. *Moeurs* is a device to add dimensions to the narrative. As such, it helps to cast doubt upon any single aspect or any single interpretation. Its work done, it is finally discarded as unreliable.

Darley is the "I" of three parts of the *Quartet*, and it is convenient to make a distinction between Darley-as-narrator and Darley-as-character. As narrator he seems most useful to Durrell-as-novelist when he bungles, when he stops and confesses that he is on the wrong track, when he admits his incompetence. In *Justine* he says: "I want to put things down simply and crudely, without style—the plaster and whitewash . . ." (*J*:83). Darley's modesty, his concessions, and his real and pretended incompetence are further devices. Darley-as-character will experience more than he can express, and Durrell-as-novelist gets nearer to the truth— which is that truth is always relative—as he assembles his battery of oblique witnesses, testimonials, paintings, letters, comments, intercalations, and interlinears: his observation posts in space-time.

As part of his exploration for the truth, Darley has recourse to many documents, such as the corrections to *Justine* made by Balthazar, known as the "Great Interlinear," and to Nessim's diaries, pages of which, he tells us, he has destroyed (*J*:208). This is not very scholarly, but the alleged destruction does limit the theoretically infinite number of possible approaches to the material. Darley is made to select and to sift the evidence. Besides, Darley tells us, he writes slowly, "with such pain" (*B*:17).

At the beginning of the second volume he has been driven back to the starting point again by Balthazar's emendations. At times he becomes eloquent in his awareness of the difficulty of his task:

"I mean that I must try and strip the opaque membrane which stands between me and the reality of their [Justine's, Pursewarden's, and Clea's] actions—and which I suppose is composed of my own limitations of vision and temperament. My envy of Pursewarden, my passion for Justine, my pity for Melissa. Distorting mirrors, all of them . . . [*sic*]" (*B*:28). Since envy, passion, and pity are distorting mirrors, and Darley himself is another distorting factor, the error of the error compounds. The more witnesses, *provided they are selected at random,* the better the chance that the aggregate testimony will approach the truth. All suborned or perjured witnesses could testify identically, and their unanimity is probable evidence of their falseness along this continuum of relativity, indeterminacy, and probability-truth.

Honest man that he tries to be, Darley broods over Balthazar's corrections and insertions. He carries the manuscript in his hand as he walks along the beach. He ponders the truth of Balthazar's charge that Darley trusts too much to what his subjects say about themselves and that he has been protecting himself from reality. He registers the pain of truth-seeking: "The wicked Interlinear, freighted with these doubts, presses like a blunt thumb, here and here, always in bruised places" (*B*:185). Darley begins to copy Balthazar's manuscript word for word. He tries to understand how it differs from his own version of the truth. And, as he reworks the first reality, he creates other layers of reality, feeling himself changing too—until he seems to change from observer and teller to finder. His admission of failure as storyteller is a boast of ultimate success.

In *Mountolive* he becomes temporarily an object being observed and must be dealt with in turn by the other narrators and interpreters. He becomes a "vaguely amiable bespectacled creature . . ." (*M*:111). As he resumes his role as chief narrator in *Clea,* Darley tells the story of his own storytelling in which he has been in danger of losing his identity; and, at the same time, he fights his way back to the original goal of finding *himself* through this process of borrowing, emending, and remembering—in order to alter truth into *truths.* He seems to ponder and theorize less, and to act more. He changes from observer to protagonist. Finally he acts in his proper self toward Clea. At this point one is done with Darley-as-technical-device and takes up with Darley-as-character, who is neither a merely amiable schoolteacher nor a brooding observer; he is a complete person whose behavior in turn has been variously misinterpreted by a number of other observers.

The other important narrator-writer, Pursewarden, is a special case of point of view, for much of the time he is already dead and has become only a remembered voice or text. Unlike Arnauti, who never appears in person, Pursewarden plays more than one role. At no point, however, has Durrell given over to him the responsibility that is attributed to Darley. Pursewarden comments, is quoted as commenting, is remembered as commenting endlessly on pretty much everything. He—or the memory of him—hangs around throughout the *Quartet*. His poetry is quoted, his trilogy (*God is a Humorist*) referred to in passing, his aphorisms and "Obiter Dicta" incorporated in the text and collected in an appendix to *Balthazar*, his letters reprinted (one of them twenty-eight pages long!), and a letter from Pursewarden to Clea copied out by Clea in her letter to Darley: "harsh and crabbed if you like, but none the less typical of our friend" (*B*:237).

Pursewarden's diary is extensively quoted from. It becomes the heart of *Clea*, containing important cross-references and comments on the past. His poem about Liza is read by Mountolive, who then understands. His suicide letters—one to Mountolive, one to Liza—give two versions of his suicide, not quite irreconcilable, but at tension one with another. In *Clea*, Darley hears Pursewarden's dead voice "like the chime of a distant bell" (*C*:41).

Darley "uses" Pursewarden the most, especially in the fourth volume—the part of the *Quartet* which has moved forward in time: "I thought of the verses . . . which Pursewarden used sometimes to recite" (*C*:269). "A phrase of Pursewarden's came into my mind . . ." (*C*:257). Darley's near-obsession with the memory of Pursewarden is more than casual; it is a means of keeping Pursewarden as a commentator alive after he has died as a character. Darley's distortions, as in a mirror, of Pursewarden's "meanings" are like reflections of reflections; they are increasingly untrustworthy but, by the same token, also increasingly imaginative and creative.

The second volume is Balthazar's book, not only in title but in method. His interlinear notes to Darley's manuscript—his "dry marginal comments"—correct the "fallacies and misapprehensions" in Darley's version of events. When at times it seems incredible that Balthazar could have known what he says he knows, he explains to Darley that he knew the characters well and discussed one with another; or that he reconstructed the facts from over-hearing a self-addressed monologue; or that, as with Pursewarden and Justine, "They corresponded through me" (*B*:125). Balthazar as privileged physician knows even more than he tells. But selecting and interpreting, Balthazar is really no more reliable than the other narrators. He adds dimensions while subtracting reliability. He adds color, new ways of looking at things, suggests new theories to explain old facts, and adds new facts to disrupt old theories.

The most interesting aspect of Balthazar-as-character in the *Quartet* is his approximation to a god. He is himself aware of his tendency to play god. As a ventriloquist he can give his utterances to others. In *Mountolive* he tells how he once "invented" a pair of lovers, with tragic consequences (*M*:234-35). As an accomplished chess player, he is an organizer of gambits and arranges moves. But he is a fallible god, one who forgives and is forgiven. In the end it is Balthazar who accidentally—and negligently—is the cause of Clea's losing a hand. Balthazar's role seems to extend into the future as he warns Darley in his last appearance in the *Quartet*: "You can't shake me off. The Wandering Jew, you know" (*C*:271).

In *Mountolive* Durrell-as-novelist speaks up now and then, generalizes, observes, comments. This voice is the "dear reader" addresser of the traditional novel in which the novelist is there to help bridge gaps and to indicate highlights and lowlights. A little word like "indeed," an adverbial modifier of an event recorded objectively, betrays the presence of the novelist. But it is only with the impact of *all* the voices that Durrell speaks clearly in the *Quartet*. Durrell's creative act is his voice.

Other narrative devices include Capodistria's letters, Clea's letters, paintings, and memories; Justine's diaries, Leila's letters, Liza's narratives, the barber's anecdotes, and Mountolive's "Notes." Capodistria's long letter—said to be written in French but printed in English in the text of the novel—is read aloud at his "grave" by Clea to Balthazar and Darley. Capodistria's "voice" from the grave in which he is not buried is mimicked by Clea, and thus versions of Capodistria's point of view, his tone, and his style are added to the story, distorted, reflected, refracted. But in the *Quartet* no one can select the *true* image in an infinite series of mirrors.

Clea's comments and letters are used liberally to vary the angle of narration, to reflect various moments in various colors. Her paintings, although not literally reproduced, are described; and her subjects, Mountolive, and Justine—the two most important ones—are seen from that perspective. Clea can lipread and thus can observe and report conversations. She is also an accomplished mimic and on suitable occasions recreates Scobie after his death. Clea's imitation of Scobie's telling a story about his friend Toby— as related by Darley in *Clea*—is far removed from the source. (Toby has little chance to speak for himself against this battery of retellers and interpreters.) Clea's final letter gives news of Mountolive, Pombal, Amaril, Justine, and others. Her assurance at this point in the story gives these accounts a kind of validity which is less convincing than it is neat. Clea is also the creator of Semira's nose, and finally she is the wielder of an artificial hand which itself can create!

Justine's "diary" (Darley mentions three volumes) and Nessim's "folio" are referred to in passing but seldom quoted from. Justine's diary was originally in French. One of the passages translated and quoted by Darley includes the remarkable description of the slaughtering of the camel in the street (*J*:61-62). Then in *Mountolive* the "truth" is told: the diaries of Justine are really notes by Arnauti for his book, which Justine copied out for him and which were never used in the book. She has passed them off to Darley as her own. But in her proper voice as teller, not forger and recounter, Justine is referred to by Balthazar as truthful. It is from her that Balthazar got the "true" version of her affair with Pursewarden.

Nessim's alleged diaries, referred to by both Balthazar and Darley, are shadowy items. Nessim is most useful as a narrator in his own voice, such as the time he "tells" Justine about past events.

Some of Leila's letters are used, such as the two to Mountolive, to interpret as well as to further action. Other long letters of hers are referred to by Balthazar as an important source of his information.

Liza fills in the background of her affair with her brother. Occasionally her comments are pertinent and informative. The *we-used-to* quality of her pronouncements is combined with prophetic vision. In her blindness she is a seer.

The barber, Mnemjian, is introduced in the first volume as the "archives of the city" (*J*:36). But his function is not really fulfilled until the fourth volume, where as messenger from Nessim to Darley he gives the needed information on important characters like Balthazar, Nessim, Pombal, and Capodistria. Other subordinate characters function similarly from time to time. Nimrod tells a story about Budgie and imitates Scobie. Pombal tells how he took Liza to see Pursewarden's old room, and a letter of his is quoted in one of Clea's letters.

Clea is frequently quoted by Balthazar and by Darley. Darley's use of Clea's tales and comments is often forcefully prefaced, leading the reader into the trap of the *one-truth-fallacy:* "Clea one night told me the truth with her own lips!" (*B*:188). Later it is revealed as not quite the truth, but *at the time* it is endorsed by narrator Darley. Clea's letters are literate, clear, and useful to the novelist. In her roles as letter writer, interpreter, painter, mimic, and lipreader, she is made to perform multiple tasks of telling. She is an important observation post—but not a stationary one.

Scobie is a delightful story teller, and he is also a favorite subject to imitate and tell *about*. Scobie creates the character Toby in the anecdotes which are later extended in Clea's imitations. Mountolive is a note-taker, but his notes are seldom quoted.

The various narrations and observations interlock and overlap, and numerous sources of information and observation posts shift the truth-references. *The Alexandria Quartet* is an experiment in truth telling in which truth is always a function of many voices and of many points of view. It is a lavish and eloquent bearing-witness by many, many witnesses to the many truths in curved, multi-dimensional space-time.

CHAPTER 6

The Alexandria Quartet *as Oracle*

Ask a working oracle questions and it answers in enigmas. Ask *The Alexandria Quartet* for its essence and it equivocates, but perhaps the answers it gives are dusty only to those too hot after certainty. The *Quartet* is *about* the city, *about* love, *about* death, and *about* truth. It is a trick done with words—and mirrors. It is as esoteric and complex as a Tarot deck. If you like, it is work to divine by.

I *Alexandria*

Alexandria is a place quickened into a character. Alexandria is a "gravitational field" (*J*:19)—a central force in the chaos of relativism. "The city, half-imagined (yet wholly real), begins and ends in us, roots lodged in our memory" (*B*:13). The pattern of the city marks its inhabitants, and the inhabitants have in turn designed the city. The relationship is hermaphroditic. Although it is not a happy place, it is always interesting: "The sexual provender which lies to hand is staggering in its variety and profusion" (*J*:14).

The power of Alexandria is mysterious. When Justine recites lines from Cavafy for Darley, he feels the "strange equivocal power of the city"—and he knows Justine "for a true child of Alexandria; which is neither Greek, Syrian nor Egyptian, but a hybrid: a joint" (*J*:27). Pursewarden also identifies Justine with Alexandria: "Justine and her city are alike in that they both have a strong flavour without having any real character" (*J*:139).

The "spirit of place" is strong in Alexandria: its inhabitants are in its power, and there is no escape. It even enters Nessim's dreams and disturbs him. But Nessim knows he will never leave Alexandria despite his impulse to escape its "sense of deracination and failure" (*J*:180). Moreover, Alexandrians are decadent and cynical. While they love and exalt their city, they also hate it; and

Alexandria responds in kind. It is an "impossible city of love and obscenity" (B:183). Darley sees the pre-war city as a series of symbols. Its inhabitants are "master-sensualists of history abandoning their bodies to mirrors . . ." (C:14). Alexandrians love masquerading. Later, from his island, he remembers his friends "as beings unconsciously made part of place, buried to the waist among the ruins of a single city, steeped in its values . . ." (B:225).

When Darley returns to Alexandria in the fourth volume, his *remembered* city contrasts with the *real*, war-infested Alexandria. But he is helped to see it afresh by Clea, who has never been in love with Alexandria. In *Mountolive* Clea refers to the city "as it really is—with its harsh, circumscribed contours and its wicked, pleasure-loving and unromantic inhabitants" (M:155). Darley, too, eventually sees Alexandria "as it must always have been—a shabby little seaport built upon a sand-reef, a moribund and spiritless backwater" (C:103). Finally, Clea likens Alexandria to "some great public urinal" (C:105).

Alexandria is a series of projections and, like all Durrell's major characters, not a simple entity. It is above all a creation.

II *Love*

"The central topic of the book is an investigation of modern love."[1] Both Freud and de Sade, from whom quotations are used as epigraphs to *Balthazar*, recognized the power and glory of sexual love. Love is an appetite which is suppressed only with danger. Sexual needs of the civilized—conditioned—organism can no longer be satisfied simply and directly, but demand elaborate and specialized techniques, symbol systems, and supplementary paraphernalia. De Sade, romantic bad-boy, fantasied ways of satisfying these special needs. And Freud, in his vision of the free man, encouraged dipping into the well of the unconscious to find what one *really* needs sexually.

The *Quartet* is full of lovers, refugees from Durrell's *The Black Book*, from Henry Miller's *Tropics*, from Proust, from de Sade, and possibly from *Fanny Hill*.[2] Sex-victims and sex-perpetrators, they have one characteristic in common. They are aware of the polyvalences of love. They are, taken as a group, a reasonably

unbiased sampling of modern lovers. That is, they have specialized, conditioned, imaginative needs.

The various characters "love" variously. Darley loves Justine,
who loves Clea, Pursewarden, Nessim, and Darley. Pursewarden
loves Justine and Liza. Liza loves Pursewarden and Mountolive,
who loves Liza—and Leila, who loves Mountolive. Nessim loves
Justine and Melissa. Narouz loves Clea, who loves Justine, Amaril,
and Darley. Almost all "have been deeply wounded in their sex"
(*J*:14).

The homosexuals, Balthazar, Scobie, and Toto, are alternately
comic and tragic figures; for homo-eroticism is a flaw that can be
exploited for its contrasts. Homo-eroticism, sterile and insecure as
it is, is not subject to the peace of fulfillment—nor to the liabilities
of fulfillment, such as tedium and children. It is a spectacular kind
of love, tending toward fancy dress, incongruity, and mimicry. It
is the sickness of Narcissus and much given to mirror-scrutiny.

Descanting upon the many kinds of love-relationships in the
Quartet are pithy and insightful "sayings" which often genuinely
sparkle, less often fall heavy upon surfeited wits. At times, and
from certain observation posts, love seems best expressed as
"ironic tenderness and silence" (*J*:42). It has "nothing to do with
sex" (*J*:48). More demandingly, love "is an absolute which takes
all or forfeits all." (*J*:105).

Shift the axes of reference and "loving is only a sort of skin-
language, sex a terminology merely" (*J*:107). Arnauti notes "how
narrowly love and friendship are related" (*J*:204). Loving may be
truer "when sympathy and not desire makes the match" (*J*:204).
Hate may be "unachieved love" (*J*:207). Love has at least four
faces, all "terrible" (*J*:238). Toto calls love a "liquid fossil"
(*B*:27).

Love resembles madness—and religious ecstasy. Sex-passion
and religious-passion merge. The bedroom becomes the chapel,
Justine's pagan mask on the wall of her boudoir becomes a station
of the cross.

Above all, love is a paradox: ". . . to love is to become besot-
ted" (*B*:57). Yet love is the "vital touchstone to a man's being"
(*B*:63). It is the only nourishment which kills: "Concentration on
the love-object and possession are the poisons" (*B*:117).

The most intricate statements about love come from Pursewarden, whose *loving* is the most anguished. Pursewarden is not homosexual, but he does sleep with his sister. Incestuous love of one's sister, which is overtly heterosexual, may be the attempt to possess oneself as a member of the opposite sex. Thus incest becomes the dramatization of complete self-renunciation. It is at once the most decadent as well as the most exalted sex behavior known to civilization.

Pursewarden, possibly rationalizing, concludes that a "helpmeet" is greater than a lover, and that "loving-kindness" is greater than passion (B:128). Sex is more "psychic" than physical to him. Darley falls back on "enigma" as the description of the love business (B:130). He is also deeply troubled by the insight that in the kinds of love known to him there has been one common quality: "Each of us, like the moon, had a dark side—could turn the lying face of 'unlove' towards the person who most loved and needed us. And just as Justine used my love, so Nessim used Melissa's. . . . One upon the back of the other, crawling about 'like crabs in a basket'" (B:131).

Polarity, tides ("the dark tides of Eros" [B:190]), enigma, paradox—suggest, as metaphors and labels, the built-in contradictions, tensions, shifts, cycles, and unreliability of the love-concept: "Aphrodite permits every conjugation of the mind and sense in love" (B:166). Clea's problem with the unsolicited love of Narouz does not seem less because of her wise insights into the love-problems of others. She tells Darley that he has loved Justine *better* because Justine has betrayed him. "The whore is man's true darling," she says (B:236). If Clea is artfully conceived early in the *Quartet* as rationalizing her own position vis-a-vis Justine, Narouz, and Darley, then perhaps her comment on "sex" in *Clea* is the resolution: "Sexual love *is* knowledge . . ." (C:113).

But there are no *single* truths about the human heart. And love, like all else, is incomprehensible without reference to its fourth dimension. Mountolive discovers that love is a function of time and that with time love can turn to disgust. *Time* is the fourth dimension of love just as it is of *space*. "Words kill love as they kill everything else" (M:48). Of the two most important activities in life—love-making and reflecting—each kills the other; for passion destroys reflection, and reflection results in words. This is the

space-time of love, a continuum along which the parts are inseparable: it is a fusion of time (the killing aspect) and space (the
body-lust aspect) for which discerning characters like Clea feel
both disgust (with reference to Narouz' love "without consent")
and respect ("sexual love is knowledge").

In the multidimensional universe of the *Quartet* love is involved
in all the dimensions. Through the eyes of lovers reality is reflected and refracted. The novelist has his fun with the situations.[3]
He probes the connotative values, explores the spectrum of over-
tones, and involves all aspects of this many-faceted love-business
in all other aspects of his story, so that the continuum-metaphor
turns from substantive to predicate. Love metamorphoses all
characters involved, and it is felt in the entire work as "moods."
Darley's three women represent "the moods of the great verb,
Love: Melissa, Justine, and Clea" (*C*:177).

Indicative, imperative, subjunctive: the statement, the command, the wish. And each mood is shatterable into refracted aspects: question and answer, question and no answer, question
alone, answer alone; and finally, perhaps, no question *and* no answer—only the quiet of Zen.

III *Death*

As metaphor and as *fact* death is neat and useful in conventional storytelling. It makes a convenient terminus. But in space-
time stories—in contrast to linear stories—death assumes many
aspects and is not necessarily terminal. When Pursewarden kills
himself, Darley poetizes: "Nor, for the purposes of this writing
has he ceased to exist; he has simply stepped into the quicksilver
of a mirror as we all must . . ." (*J*:118). Even after death Pursewarden remains an important character, stepping into and *out of*
the mirror at the novelist's will. His death is a device to give him
importance. Darley says: ". . . the presence of death always re-
freshes experience . . . that is its function: to help us deliberate
on the novelty of time" (*J*:118). Pursewarden's death "provided a
new critical referent" (*J*:168). "It appears that death is a relative
question" (*J*:218). Capodistria is presumably killed at the duck
shoot. One learns later that his death was faked. Thus Capodistria
himself could anticipate a faked death—a strictly relative death,
as it were.

LAWRENCE DURRELL

To man the *prospect* of death is more surely an awareness than death itself, especially the prospect of one's own death. So the main value of the concept "death" is psychological. It is, as a concept, most useful *before* and *after* the event of death, not during the event. "It is hard to know how to behave with the dead," says Darley, alone with the corpse of Melissa: "One becomes awkward as if in the presence of royalty" (*J*:238). The memory of Melissa, and the echoes of Pursewarden's voice and writings, from the far side of death, become important *later*.

"The best retorts always come from beyond the grave" (*B*:20). Pursewarden's death, Darley feels, perhaps "actually enriched our [Justine's and Darley's] own love-making" (*B*:223). In space-time, where time comes and goes in spirals and cycles, a memory does not decrease in intensity as any simple linear function. It comes and goes in bursts of renewed energy and vividness. Some dead people become more and more memorable the "longer" they are dead. But eventually, in all-space-time, everything must be "refunded into silence" (*B*:242). Paradoxically, death is both negation and incentive—and also aphrodisiac. Clea sees Justine as "death-propelled" (*M*:197). Nessim and Justine make love better when threatened: "How thrilling, sexually thrilling, was the expectation of their death!" (*M*:206).

The cathartic function of death is dramatically set forth in the Coptic wake for Narouz: "In this way the whole grief of the countryside was refunded once again into living, purged of bitterness, reconquered by the living through the dead image of Narouz" (*M*:317). By heightening tensions the presence of death, the expectation of death, and the memory of death—all become a *way* toward higher truths: ". . . death heightens every tension and permits us fewer of the half-truths by which we normally live" (*C*:21). In the "presence of death" kisses are "charged with . . . affirmation" (*C*:96).

The seven dead sailors with whom Clea and Darley swim in the final underwater scene are "friendly." The confounding of the *now* and the *then* and the *will-be* in space-time as one curves around the spiral, only apparently going up or down and back or forth, exalts the concept of death. In space-time the dead are everywhere as well as always.

[102]

IV *Mirrors and Prisms*

Durrell's use of mirrors is significant—not casual. Mirror imagery pervades the *Quartet*, beginning almost at once in the first volume. Cohen is glimpsed by Darley in a mirror, and at that moment Darley pities him and understands him. Justine studies herself in the five mirrors at her dressmaker's, seeing five aspects of herself. Darley and Justine "meet" in the same mirror in which Arnauti met his Claudia. Darley speaks to Pombal's head reflected in the barber-shop mirror. Melissa frequently stares at herself in mirrors, and reference is made to her "fragile mirror-worship" (*J:*54). And Justine often combs her "dark head" as she speaks to herself in the mirror. Both Nessim and Darley speak to their mirror images. Arnauti reads the blotting-paper image of one of Claudia's letters in a mirror, and he often confronts his face in mirrors. When Pursewarden dies, he is said to have "stepped into the quicksilver of a mirror" (*J:*118), and Darley remembers him as a "reflection liquefying in the mirror" (*J:*119).

Mirror images have personalities of their own. One mirror reflects "a vestigial image of a young Justine—like the calcimined imprint of a fern in chalk: the youth she believes she has lost" (*J:*136). Melissa has a cracked mirror in which the image of Selim delivering Nessim's message "blistered and flickered in the dancing gas-jets like a spectre from the underworld" (*J:*199).

Mirrors provide a second self, and they are repositories of memories. The epigraph to *Balthazar* (from de Sade) explores the image: "The mirror sees the man as beautiful, the mirror loves the man; another mirror sees the man as frightful and hates him; and it is always the same being who produces the impressions." [4] And early in the second volume Darley speaks of "memory which catches sight of itself in a mirror" (*B:*14). Characters continue to meet in the mirrors in the barber shop. Darley's envy, passion, and pity are called "distorting mirrors" (*B:*28). Scobie examines his reflection in the mirror "with complacence" (*B:*30).

Both Leila, after her disfiguring illness, and Narouz—disfigured all his life—abhor and avoid mirrors. Leila will on occasion consult a small pocket mirror, but Narouz cannot bear to see his face "even in a shaving-mirror" (*B:*94). Pursewarden curses himself in the mirror, talks to himself in the mirror, and writes messages with his shaving stick on mirrors, and at his death "every mirror bore a soap-inscription" (*B*:150).

At the carnival ball at the Cervonis the revellers in dominoes are "comparing their identical reflections . . . in the two swollen mirrors among the palms" (*B*:198-99). And later the palms themselves splinter "in the shivering mirrors" (*B*:233). In the critical scene between Narouz and his father, the father points a pistol at his own image in the mirror.

Mountolive is no less peopled with mirror images. On the very first page the world is "mirrored in a soap-bubble" (*M*:11). And the usual functions of mirrors are given the by-now familiar extra significance of self-searching. The young Mountolive talks to himself as he shaves. He goes to embrace Leila, "stumbling forward like a man into a mirror," and the meeting of "their muttering images" is compared to "reflections on a surface of lake-water" (*M*:28).

There are mirrors in almost every room in Durrell-land. Sir Louis finds much company in his mirror. He whistles "dispiritedly at his own reflection in the great mirror." Later he shouts in the bathroom "into the small mirror on the wall . . ." (*M*:76). Mountolive often ties his tie carefully, speaks to himself earnestly, catches sight of his own grandeur casually—in assorted mirrors. He is usually pleased at what he sees; he is an inveterate mirror-looker.

At the end of the third volume, after Narouz' death, the mirrors in the house are shattered into a thousand fragments.

In *Clea* mirrors are associated with Alexandria: in the shops one can buy little "lucky mirrors" and mirrors to put in birdcages to make birds sing. And significant reference is made to "master-sensualists of history abandoning their bodies to mirrors" (*C*:14). The familiar characters go on addressing themselves in mirrors, alternately admiring and despising what they see there. Pombal and Balthazar speak to their reflections, and Balthazar says, "I cursed myself in the mirror" (*C*:68). Darley recounts how Scobie, on his birthday, admired his "wrinkled" body in the mirror (*C*:88). On Clea's face comes that "look of complicity which women reserve only for their mirrors" (*C*:99). Pursewarden calls the writer's ego-problems "Mirror-worship" (*C*:110).

Perhaps the ultimate use of mirror imagery comes when the

blind Liza seems to scan a mirror for her own image: "*This caged reflection gives her nothing back/That women drink like thirsty stags from mirrors*" (C:189).

In the *Quartet,* imagery of the "prism" is related in tone and use to mirror imagery. References to the different "faces of the prism" extend the metaphors of refraction, changing patterns, and shifting light. At dusk Alexandria is "stained with colours as if from a shattered prism . . ." (B:152). Reality is seen best as refracted and analyzed through a prism. Street lamps can become "prismatic lights," and visitors to Memlik's palace are changed into "harlequins" by the light coming through the "coloured fanlights in cheap cathedral glass" (M:258). The city sometimes spreads "the sticky prismatic wings of a new-born dragon fly on the night" (C:91).

Darley fears that as narrator he lacks clear vision. For him "truth" is refracted by his own personality "disorders" (C:107). But Pursewarden elsewhere says that "human personality seen across a continuum would perhaps become prismatic" (C:135-36), So Darley is an adequate observer *because* he refracts, not *despite* the fact. In Durrell's space-time novel, mirrors and prisms reflect and refract the various aspects of reality as devices for improving and sharpening vision.

V *Masks and Blindness*

Durrell's use of masks and blindness is also not casual. The mask is disguise, an assumed appearance; and blindness is the ultimate masking of perception.

In the *Quartet* stark blindness is reserved for Liza, partial blindness, half-vision, and distorted vision for others. Nessim is finally half-blinded, and Justine's eye droops after her stroke. The decorative Tibetan mask which hangs in Justine's bedroom is blind. The holes for the eyes light up, but they do not record what they reflect. The many mirrors are blind. They reflect without perceiving. The face in the mirror is as blind as a mask.

At the end of *Justine* Nessim has not changed *inside:* "He had merely adopted a new mask" (J:241). So Darley says; but Darley is also partially blind, psychologically. He resolves in the beginning to try to "strip the opaque membrane" which has obstructed his vision of the actions of the characters about whom he writes.

Finally, however, his search for *fact* emerges as a kind of blindness.

In relativity land, where *appearance* and authority are both unreliable, sightlessness—the seal set upon the eyes—may be sacred. Clea is made to experience this kind of blindness relative to her perception of Justine: "So great was her confusion of mind that she would sit and stare at the metamorphosed Justine and try to remember what she really looked like on the other side of the transforming membrane, the cataract with which Aphrodite seals up the sick eyes of lovers, the thick, opaque form of a sacred sightlessness" (*B*:54).

Justine, as in disguise, has been transformed by Clea's love. Just as the velvet domino bestows anonymity on the wearer at a carnival, allowing freedom of action because the beholder can not *see* who is behind the disguise, so blindness bestows freedom of action on those the blind can not see. The sleeping mask, producing blessed night at high noon, is more than an escape device. It is a means to the truth of relativity. Appearance is truth—relatively speaking.

At carnival time Narouz has no harelip, Semira has no no-nose. Pursewarden's death mask and the Tibetan mask on Justine's bedroom wall both tolerate in absolute composure what they "see." Blinded canaries will sing more passionately, for they are not distracted. Unblinded canaries are fooled with mirrors into singing to their images in the little mirrors.

At times Justine's face is as "expressionless as a mask of Siva" (*M*:206). An old blind sheik presides over Memlik's "night of God," and his blindness suggests holiness. Scobie has a glass eye. Hamid is one-eyed. Abdul, finally, is almost blind. The child of Liza and Pursewarden was born blind. An organ grinder named Arif is blind. Even Hamid's brother is a blind muezzin. The acrobats wear masks and painted faces, and the faces of the child prostitutes are painted masks. And even Semira's new nose, the new created image, is only a disguise.

A series of masquerading masqueraders is reflected in an infinite series of mirrors. Reality is finally the awareness of the lack of reality. The blind may see more clearly. This is the oracle's equivocal answer: a trick done with mirrors—and words.

VI *Words*

Durrell uses many words and many different kinds of words in the *Quartet*. He uses rare words—words of low frequency of occurrence in the everyday language—more often than most writers do. He likes certain words. He finds them effective, and so he uses them. Also, he uses words at unexpected places. But he is never really obscure. It may be necessary to look up such words as *acedia, anfract, banausic,* and *burk* (as a verb). One may not be sure about *chitou* and *chthonian* (the latter, Darley says, is Pursewarden's "favourite word"). Words like *cicisbeo, dimorphism, fatidic,* and *gravid* are appropriate in their contexts. Other examples of Durrell's fancier words would be useful in an advanced spelling bee: *hebetude, hypnagogic, khamseen, laic, menhir, phthisic, sancing, sistrum, subfusc,* and *vernissage.*

The *Quartet* is awash with color words, "sequences of tempora" like "dust-red, dust-green, chalk-mauve and watered crimson-lake" (*J*:14), and "the colours that memory gives . . ." (*B*:140). There are sunlight colors: at dawn "the first overflow of citron and rose" (*C*:26). Later, there are twilight colors; "umbrageous violet" (*C*:259). There are Levantine colors: "gold and reds of oranges" and "slips of magenta"; and the colors of Justine: rouge on her face, gold on her nails, mauve on her lips. There are underwater colors: "from emerald to apple green, and from Prussian blue to black" (*C*:226).

White and black are fundamentals: the white city, the white towers, and the black water. And then blue—a favorite color: a "handful of blue days" in *Clea* (13), the sunlight on the blue water, the blue lights of the city, the "metallic blue of carbon paper" streets (*M*:160), and always the blue Alexandrian twilight, the "little blue hands" on the walls of the brothel (*C*:147), the blue marker buoy in the harbor, and the blue eyes: Narouz' "sky-blue eyes of a girl," Clea opening her blue eyes, the blue eyes of the reporter Keats—and finally the "blue-fires" of the sex act between Justine and Nessim.

Durrell has a tendency to drop names—a defensible device in textured prose. A concordance to famous names alluded to in the *Quartet* would serve no purpose, for the work is not a learned treatise; but as an example of the eclecticism of the references certain items are interesting. An index would range from *Augustine, Auden, Aquinas, Blake, Bonnard, Byron, Chaucer, Claudel, Coleridge, Demonax, Descartes, Dickens,* and *Donne* through *Paracelsus, Patmore, Petrarch, Petronius, Plotinus, Pope,* and *Proust* ending with *Stendhal, Swedenborg, Tolstoy, Trollope, Whitman,* and *Wordsworth.*

The Alexandria Quartet is made of words, artfully dropped and for the most part magnificently cadenced. The tendency toward abundance is reassuring. No carping editor or over-solicitous friend seems to have cut or moderated this word stream. It flows generously. It seeks the sea-level of Truth.[5]

VII *Truth*

There is, of course, no one, single truth in a space-time novel. "Everything is true of everybody" (*B*:140). Pursewarden quotes (or rather *misquotes*) Coventry Patmore: "The truth is great and will prevail/When none care whether it prevail or not." [6] Furthermore, such truth must be apprehended carelessly.

Depth psychology justifies considering slips of the tongue as more nearly valid indexes of truth than consciously controlled utterances. But there is no end to the mazes and labyrinths involved in this kind of reasoning. First of all, the reasoning per se is subject to the fallacies of all controlled utterances—and truth that can prevail only when it is *unaware,* has no ready means of ascertaining when the *significant* slip of the tongue has been made. Ultimately, truth hunting becomes an absurdity—or a game.

In *Balthazar,* the volume in which the "*facts*" as presented in *Justine* are altered and emended, truth hunting becomes the game of "all is relative." Pursewarden, whose mysterious suicide is one of the spectacular examples of multi-faceted truth in the *Quartet,* felt his own life was often following the "curvature" of his stories: "Reality . . . was always trying to copy the imagination of man, from which it derived" (*B*:116). Thus life, an imitation of art, leads back to art, an imitation of life—in endless cycles and spirals. Science justifies repudiating itself as an influence on reality rather than a description of reality. Intuition, irony, and obliqueness—these are the ways to truth: "Truth is independent of fact. It does not mind being disproved. It is already dispossessed in utterance" (*B*:246).

Balthazar teaches Darley the truth about facts: "Each fact can have a thousand motivations, all equally valid, and each fact a thousand faces" (*C*:72-73). It would seem, then, that irony is the only tone proper to the attempt to tell the truth. Thus Pursewarden identifies Jesus as an ironist, even as a comedian: "I am sure that two-thirds of the Beatitudes are jokes or squibs in the manner of Chuang Tzu. Generations of mystagogues and pedants have lost the sense. I am sure of it however because he must have known that Truth disappears with the telling of it. It can only be conveyed, not stated; irony alone is the weapon for such a task" (*C*:144).

If Durrell-as-novelist is an ironist, then the statements about the difficulty of conveying truth must be taken as part of the *conveying*. They are additional devices—and since the wrong approach to the Beatitudes may be to take them seriously, the wrong approach to Durrell's novel may be to *believe* the comments on the work in the work except as they call attention to the paradox that what they say cannot be done is being done precisely as they say it cannot be done. The saying of the undoableness furthers the doing of it, making the work an honest deception, an admitted lie, in which all narrators are unreliable—including the novelist himself. All is paradox.

Pursewarden is the specialist in paradox: "Words being what they are, people being what they are, perhaps it would be better always to say the opposite of what one means" (*C*:134). And, when Pursewarden practices this theory, what he means is the opposite of what he says, and thus he does not mean the theory at all. If God Himself is an Ironist, there is no way out of this big-scale joke. The theory of relativity becomes the laughter of God. Reality is a joke.

The impossibility of becoming an artist—the prerequisite is to shed those very qualities, such as egotism, that lead to the decision to become an artist—is called by Pursewarden "The Whole Joke" (*C*:128). It is in his sharp remarks to Darley (as Brother Ass) that Pursewarden reaches both heights and depths, as he himself recognizes, taking himself furiously seriously and unseriously. His passion and his confusion have dramatic value; they reach beyond reason to the paradox, and there he finds his rationalizations and justifies himself—with a smile. Of T. S. Eliot,

Pursewarden says: "His honesty of measure and his resolute bravery to return to the headsman's axe is a challenge to us all; but where is the smile?" (*C*:134).

The smile may be Durrell's experiment in the space-time novel. The smile may hover over the solemn critical evaluations of the experiment. Like many creative people, Durrell lightly scorns the academic critic. His close friendship with Henry Miller has been reinforced by their shared indifference to academia. Pursewarden refers to "our older universities where they are still painfully trying to extract from art some shadow of justification for their way of life. Surely there must be a grain of hope, they ask anxiously?" (*C*:134).

Charged by Balthazar with being "equivocal," Pursewarden utters his paradoxical and ironic dicta on truth, words, and people "without a moment's conscious thought"—always the sign of an honest answer in Freud-land. The basic technique of irony is saying the opposite of what one means—without hesitation. There is, then, an appalling possibility that the way to write a conventional novel *ironically* is to announce boldly that one is writing a completely unconventional one!

"The object of writing is to grow a personality which in the end enables man to transcend art" (*B*:141). So the "whole joke" includes the fact that, once the writing is transmuted into a miracle, the object of the miracle is to enable man to get along without the miracle. This is an appropriate comment on a universe created by a Deity who is so powerful (and whimsical) that He does not need to exist.

To Pursewarden, only the artist makes things happen, and society should be founded on him. Art, in the "arty" sense, exists for the critics alone. In *Clea*—the volume that disappointed the art-seeking critics the most—Pursewarden is dead but Darley emerges as a healthy, muscular, *knows-where-he's-been-and-where-he's-going fellow.* He is receptive to the Henry Miller-Pursewarden kind of advice (passed on to him by Clea): ". . . tell your ego to go to hell and not make a misery of what should be essentially *fun, joy*" (*C*:110).

Pursewarden defines "good art" as a "pointer" only:

Good art points, like a man too ill to speak, like a baby! But if instead of following the direction it indicates you take it for a thing in itself, having some sort of absolute value, or as a thesis upon something which can be paraphrased, surely you miss the point; you lose yourself at once among the barren abstractions of the critic? [*sic*] Try to tell yourself that its fundamental object was only to invoke the ultimate healing silence—and that the symbolism contained in form and pattern is only a frame of reference through which, as in a mirror, one may glimpse the idea of a universe at rest, a universe in love with itself. Then like a babe in arms you will "milk the universe at every breath"! We must learn to read between the lines, between the lives. (*C*:142-43)

But Pursewarden's voice is only one of many. True, his voice is the most memorable and quotable, and thus he skews the work in his direction. Yet Pursewarden is not the hero.

In *The Alexandria Quartet* the reader has been exalted, mortified, and educated by turns. After a certain time, varying for each reader, he no longer responds at the highest intensity levels. He has been worn down. There is no reason for assuming that such an effect was not planned by the novelist, for it *all* adds up. The total work may emerge as a kind of joke on the joke, in which the reader, trained to expect irony, is fooled by the intermittent and erratic seriousness and solemnity (of the last volume, for example) into accepting the work literally. The usual reaction has been to call the non-ironic parts inferior.[7] The effect may, however, be predictable and artful. After so many devices, the only new device that will move the reader is a *decrease* in devices—or something as simple as old-fashioned melodrama.

Certainly Durrell's claim that he based his four-decker novel on the relativity proposition in order to give it the unities that modern literature has lacked is no mere empty boast. Evidence within the work shows definite responses to the relativity proposition as understood in descriptive and metaphorical terms. These responses are seen mainly in *increases* in techniques that make for various points of view rather than for the invention of new techniques per se. The manipulating of time sequences and the references to time—and related imagery—are also increased significantly with the result that patterns within the work are complicated, truth is elusive, perhaps always ironically and paradoxically stated. Linearity of all kinds—except the basic linearity of word after word, page after page typical of all literature—is thrown in doubt. Multiplicity rules. Characters tend to be seen as events which occur at the focus of forces rather than as stable personalities. There is an abundance of overlapping and inter-weaving.

Durrell's claim that his work is not "Proustian or Joycean [in] method" seems justified. The *increase* in confusion and uncer-tainty, so that *the* truth, for example, about Justine is never to be really known, *is* Durrell's experiment. It is the recognition of the fact, today's fact, that facts are relations, not fixed items. Indeter-minacy and relativity have urged the novel toward a kind of self-conscious decadence in its awareness of the impossibility of doing what it is doing.

CHAPTER 7

The Funny Books

TWO collections of sketches in Durrell's "Wodehouse manner" have been dignified by book form: *Stiff Upper Lip* and
Esprit de Corps—now available in one volume.[1] They are adver-
tised on the book cover as "Outrageous Spoofs of Life among the
Diplomats." As a matter of fact, diplomatic life (with or without
capitals) is seldom *really* funny, for too much is at stake. War and
peace, the ultimates in diplomacy, are too big for laughter. But, if
one alters the angle of observation, diplomacy can be very funny.
Pomposity in a *real* king, Pope, or ambassador is scandalous,
sometimes dangerous; but in *fiction* the issues and protagonists
are reduced to spoofable size—and the fun is measured in insouciance.

I   Esprit de Corps

In *Esprit de Corps*, Durrell's Antrobus is "a regular of the career." He is a narrative device with whom the "I" talks over old
times, and he is literate enough to tell what he remembers and
intelligent enough to remember well. His normalized personality
and his reasonable wit (he can't be too dull, for he has to discover
the humor in the situations) is reassuring. Nothing violent like
real war or peace intrudes to spoil the fun.

To many English and Americans, the Balkan countries such as
Yugoslavia, where Durrell served in the Diplomatic Corps, are
musical comedy settings. In the first sketch in the volume, Antrobus tells the story of a Serbian "Liberation Day" special train
which is decorated for the occasion in creaky super-ornamen-
tation. The account is wildly and innocently exaggerated, yet
grounded in the commonplace. The engineers on the special train
look like "Dostoyevsky's publishers" (14). The simile disarms. Its
outrageous stereotopy is also precise, for hairy Russians do look

like Dostoyevsky's publishers. The success of such humor, close to "corn" as it is, depends upon reader cooperation: a friendly willingness to go along with the easy and spontaneous—and the far-fetched and contrived. Other Serbs are called the "Karamazov brothers"(17).

In the next sketch the deterioration of Ambassador Polk-Mowbray, who is disgustingly Americanized by a Carrie Potts while on a mission in the "States," begins with his leaving the "u" out of words like "colour." His references to a book by Damon Runyon, a Rotary meeting, and the American "I.Q." climax in his drinking a "coke" with his spaghetti. Antrobus sighs: "In Coca-Cola veritas what?"(27).

In the next sketch there is fun with typographical errors. The old ladies who "edit" the *Balkan Herald* get medals after years of misspelling and malaproping, such as "THE BALKAN HERALD KEEPS THE BRITISH FLAG FRYING" (29). The fun requires responses to "Big Bun" [*sic*] and "Wetminster Abbey" [*sic*]. The headline that announces that the Queen of Holland is giving a "panty" for ex-servicemen is typical of the syndrome. It is all jolly —and gently tossed-off. Although Wodehouse and Thurber are contrived and profound by turns, Durrell-as-humorist is pure, sweet "corn."

There's the time poor Polk-Mowbray swallows a moth. There's the time Edgar Albert Ponting, "pigeon-chested and with longish arms"(45) pushes the British Empire downhill. One shouldn't make fun of physical eccentricities, and moth-swallowing per se isn't funny. But when pigeon-chests push the empire downhill and ambassadors swallow moths, it's only a story. And one laughs, then realizes that such fictions have a therapeutic effect: they are humbling.

The story of the Kawaguchis who have to drink Scotch whiskey ("white man's milk") instead of their customary *saki* and as a result dance a waltz without knowing how to dance and end up in the pond into which sewage drains, is unabashedly slapstick, college-level. But the reader forgives—because Durrell so fully expects him to forgive him his simple sophistication, typed with one finger in twenty minutes.[2]

The embassy butler, Drage, is a "strange, craggy Welsh Baptist with long curving arms as hairy as a Black Widow"(63). The "Third Secretary," De Mandeville, has his hair waved-and-set once a month. And "Butch" Benbow, naval attaché, severs a tow rope tied to a populated raft, with dire consequences. The party on the liberated raft drift down stream, and once again pomp is humbled, pretentiousness discounted.

The second-last sketch in the American edition tells of the French ambassadress, called "La Valise," known privately to the members of the corps as "The Diplomatic Bag extraordinary," who turns into a male. A little heavy, this one!

The last sketch, "Cry Wolf" is built on a game invented by Wormwood: "I am imagining that I am in a sleigh with the whole Diplomatic Corps. We are rushing across the steppes, pursued by wolves. It is necessary, as they keep gaining on us, to throw a diplomat overboard from time to time in order to let the horses regain their advantage. Who would you throw first . . . and then second . . . and then third . . . ? Just look around you" (102). It's a game anyone can play as fantasy. Later Wormwood plays the game for real. The spirit of the corps is good!

And Durrell, too, has enjoyed throwing a diplomat overboard now and then.

II Stiff Upper Lip

In *Stiff Upper Lip* the "Antrobus File" continues; it has still the thinnest of frameworks, but it is adequate for light humor. A weekly lunch with Antrobus at his club is followed by reminiscences about "old times in the Foreign Service." Antrobus, still a good rememberer, thinks back to "Vulgaria" and Polk-Mowbray, under whom he served, and to De Mandeville, over whom he served. When De Mandeville is convicted, in the first sketch, of putting garlic in the embassy food, the absolution is chlorophyl. Antrobus elevates the trivial to tragedy, then lightly resolves the tragic-trivial impasse. This is the *ritual* of humor. As the comic muse, Antrobus looks up and looks down. Equally at ease with superiors and inferiors, he is the spirit of light moments in heavy days.

Stiff Upper Lip, like its predecessor, *Esprit de Corps*, tosses off the moment of truth carelessly. One who reads these little fun-rituals in one sitting, chewing wafer after wafer of pure cornbread, may blame only himself if the taste palls; for these sketches should be nibbled, not gulped.

In the next sketch, the diplomats' over-sampling of the "Vulgarian's" wines (the occasion being the launching of some twenty new wines on the market) gets somehow mixed with Dovebasket's attraction to Polk-Mowbray's niece, Angela. The incident ends in drunken slapstick. After the disaster, Polk-Mowbray says: "And remember that in Peace, in War, in Love and in Diplomacy one thing is needful. I do not, I think, need to tell you what that is"(27). (Of course, it's a stiff upper lip.)

Antrobus does not believe in "Sport." Polk-Mowbray does. The result is predictable—a near war between British and Italian Missions as the result of a recreational football match. In this kind of humor little tensions precipitate crises, and serious conflicts dwindle to little contretemps as the humorist distorts the variables and rearranges the outlines of the issues to fit an eccentric personality or a well-meaning bungler.

What happens to Mungo Piers-Foley, military attaché, "one of those mournful cylindrical men with hair parted in the middle— men who say little but think a lot" is also predictable (39). Inadvertently having eaten horse meat, he is forced by his conscience to resign; for he is a member of "The Society for the Prevention of Everything to Nags." Later he deteriorates, eats octopus, then elephant, then hallucinates "Leeches *à la rémoulades*" and other delicacies made from snakes and rats.

Polk-Mowbray, as master of insouciance, is "subject to Sudden Urges" which include keeping bees. The story of the bee and the ambassador is a study in contrasts: little-but-with-a-sting and big-but-stingless. It is entitled "Where the Bee Sucks. . . ." It could have been worse: "To Bee or not to Bee," for example!

In the next sketch, Trevor Dovebasket, assistant military attaché, is accused of compacting with the devil. Dovebasket's eyebrows meet in the middle. He bites his nails. The climax comes when Dovebasket's "inaudible whistle" has a marked effect on the ambassador's "Diplomatic Dog Show." After that Dovebasket departs. He is promoted "upwards."

Here is a world in which stiffness and charm conflict, one in which imaginativeness wins a kind of ironic victory disguised as defeat. It is a world in which, according to Antrobus in the next sketch, "people called Percy are almost invariably imbeciles" (65). And when Percy is a second footman, anything can happen —and of course it does. This sketch is, however, *really* too elementary. Involving trouble with a suit of armor, it does not transmute into pure gold. It's just not funny.

"The Swami's Secret" returns to "Butch" Benbow, the naval attaché who has "definite leanings towards the occult." He is threatened with a visit from his swami. He is anxious: "A loincloth is a tricky thing in diplomacy" (75). The swami, called Veranda, arrives fully dressed, however. Every bit a gentleman, he charms the corps; then he cleans them out, stealing artfully and smoothly. But Veranda's disproportions are not discomfiting to pretensions. The sketch is confusing. His thievery is a dirty trick in earnest— and produces few chuckles.

In the last sketch (American edition) a "smircher" is himself smirched: justice is done. Antrobus is seen in action. This time he is not merely reminiscing. Committing his first felony, he punctures the tires (all four of them) of the Rolls of Toby Imhof, the press officer who had besmirched *The Times*.

Antrobus in action, enjoying his athletic victory, is a fitting ending to this sequence of tales-that-seem-twice-told about things and people who stumble and stutter over their own vanities or obstruct the free flow of fancy and charm. *Here* the British Empire only totters a bit. It *really* fell for reasons other than the foibles of Polk-Mowbray and the inanities of the attachés. But perhaps it fell not with a bang but with a chuckle—keeping a stiff upper lip.

CHAPTER 8

The Travel Books

D URRELL is not a traveler. He is a writer who has lived in
several places which he has written about. The distinction
underlines the difference between writing manufactured by travelers who take notes (or note-takers who travel) and Durrell's
delightful accounts of interesting places. However, the category
"travel books" is convenient (for librarians) and unambiguous
(for readers).

Durrell has written three "island books" and many articles and
sketches classifiable as non-fiction. Most of his non-fiction is either
funny or "educational." Of the latter, the travel-writing is the most
important. The island books and a series of articles which appeared in *Holiday* magazine are reviewed in this chapter as representative of Durrell's best in this medium.[1]

It has taken twenty-five years for almost all the tourists to discover almost all the accessible islands, and Durrell's writing has
contributed in general to the world-wide island boom and in particular to the popularity of the so-called "Greek islands." His enthusiasm is genuine, and his Corfu-Rhodes-Cyprus books are un-
affected by anything more stylistically difficult than intense lyrical
moments. Although literate and fastidious, they are easy to read.

It is customary to refer good Durrell writing to the poet in him
—as if poetic talent always motivates fine prose; but a professional writer cares little whether it is the poet in him which makes
him write vivid prose or his prosaic quality which results in flat
poetry. Durrell writes both clear and obscure poetry, both high
and low prose. The travel books are not merely little chips off the
poetic continuum. They are authentic aspects of the professional
Durrell.[2]

I Prospero's Cell

The first of the island books, *Prospero's Cell*, opens innocently and beautifully: "Somewhere between Calabria and Corfu the blue really begins" (11). The little book proceeds in an orderly fashion. Each section is dated. The time spanned is from April 4, 1937, through September 20, 1938. Although chronology is respected, dreams are confounded with reality: "It is a sophism to imagine that there is any strict dividing line between the waking world and the world of dreams. N. and I, for example, are confused by the sense of several contemporaneous lives being lived inside us; the sensation of being mere points of reference for space and time" (11-12). For the curious, "N." is Durrell's first wife, Nancy. Durrell also acknowledges the realness of several other characters in the book: "Theodore Stephanides, Zarian, The Count D., and Max Nimiec." Scholarly sources are also accredited.

Prospero's Cell is an affectionately written book. It has the fine professional carelessness of controlled but uncramped writing in which the writer's reach does not exceed his grasp. The "account" begins in April as Durrell takes a fisherman's house at Kalamai: "A white house set like a dice on a rock already venerable with the scars of wind and water" (12). There he writes in a room overhung with cypress and olive trees. He wears his charm gracefully —and modestly implies that his pleasant situation is a function of luck rather than wit. Yet much effort and some intelligence engineered the move to Corfu.[3]

Corfu: "World of black cherries, sails, dust, arbutus, fishes and letters from home" (20). The dream-reality begins. Life is good. By September, 1937, Durrell writes: "Our life on this promontory has become like some flawless Euclidean statement. Night and sleep resolve and complete the day with their *quod erat demonstrandum* . . ." (34).

Durrell is liberal with the palette, and his ear is excellent: color, sound, light, shadow, and rhythm. The moods and tones of *Prospero's Cell* can not be summarized, but certain facts emerge in the telling. Tradition makes Corfu the home of the Phaecians and the place where Ulysses met Nausicaa. Also Corfu was possibly the island home of Shakespeare's Prospero—and of Judas Iscariot, whose descendant is a shoemaker in the village. Of such stuff are travel books made on. The essence of this book, however, is the island dream—and a generous flow of words and wine.

In the end, the war comes: "The day war was declared we stood on the balcony of the white house in a green rain falling straight down out of heaven on to the glassy floor of the lagoon; we were destroying papers and books, packing clothes, emptying cupboards, both absorbed in the inner heart of the dark crystal, and as yet not conscious of separation" (133).

The simple adjectives *white, green, glassy, dark,* and the unadorned sentiment combine to illuminate the heart of the crystal. This is good writing. And even better writing will follow.

II Reflections on a Marine Venus

The second island book, *Reflections on a Marine Venus,* is sometimes considered inferior to the first and third island books— but such ranking is unfortunate if not myopic. One reviewer said the "elements" were there, but "as sometimes happens to mayonnaise, they have not quite coalesced." [4] A book, however, is not a salad dressing. Perhaps it need not coalesce like good mayonnaise.

Durrell wrote:

This book is by intention a sort of anatomy of islomania, with all its formal defects of inconsequence and shapelessness: of conversations begun and left hanging in the air: of journeys planned and never undertaken: of notes and studies put together against books unwritten. . . . [*sic*] It is to be dedicated to the resident goddess of a Greek island—Rhodes. I should like, if possible, to recall some part of those golden years, whose ghosts still use up and afflict me whenever I catch sight of a letter with a Greek stamp on it, or whenever, in some remote port of the world, I happen upon a derelict tanker flying the Aegean blue-and-white. (16)

For the "common reader" this book is glamor. And its "formal defects" are the realism which both tempers and heightens the effect. The book fulfills its function with distinction and dignity.

Durrell's technique is eclectic: ". . . sifting into the material now some old notes from a forgotten scrap-book, now a letter: all the quotidian stuff which might give a common reader the feeling of life lived in a historic present" (16). And it works.

Rhodes, in the Durrell-adventure known as his life, comes after Alexandria and before his assignments in Argentina, Yugoslavia, and Cyprus. It is an important between-time: the time in which the Alexandrian material begins to change from experience-as-living to memory and then back again to experience-as-writing.

In Rhodes Durrell is "accredited to the occupying forces as Information Officer" (24). Characteristically, he makes many friends. Among them, Gideon is a gently delinquent officer eventually going to Palermo: Hoyle, the British Consul, is "small and rotund, with a large head and luminous eye" (32). He knows nine languages. Mills is a young doctor with an Italian sports car, a "born healer" in the presence of whom one felt ashamed of being ill. Huber is a potter who lives in a Martello tower like Stephen's in *Ulysses*. Mehmet, Durrell's neighbor, returns from a secret trip to Turkey every month with contraband. A young man named Christ discovers he is a writer when Durrell orders a column of his printed in the paper Durrell is supervising. Christ's friends are impressed: "There is nothing like cold print for commanding the respect of the ordinary." And thus Christ enters "the most impoverished aristocracy in the world" (58).

During the fine days of "the little summer of St. Demetrius" Durrell visits the other islands in his "parish": Symi, Kalymnos, Cos, Leros, Patmos. Returning from Patmos, Durrell sees a "poor wretch in a leaky boat, half-naked, setting out lobster pots." The wash of the bigger boat passing "sets him bouncing"—but Durrell does not curse: ". . . in a flash I see the Greece I love again: the naked poverty that brings joy without humiliation, the chastity and fine manners of the islanders, the schisms and treacheries of the townsmen, the thrift and jealousy of the smallholders. I see the taverns with their laurel wreaths, the lambs turning on the spit at Easter, the bearded heroes, the shattered marble statutes" (76).

Now thousands of tourists who cruise the islands looking for what Durrell and his friends discovered there often forget that those earlier romantics were never deluded. The pioneers saw the venality and the poverty. They were romantic in that they felt the poverty had dignity, but they did not sentimentalize. They paid honest attention to experience and did not under-estimate the guts and labor it takes to convert that experience into literature. They also respected the past.

A chapter on the history of Rhodes is included. History is described as "that vast complex of analogies" (80). So defined, history includes fact and fancy, lore and myth. Thus Pan, who still lives in much of Greece, is reported as having been seen in Rhodes. (He is called there a *Kaous*.) To Durrell, Pan and history constantly hover in the background. The foreground is occupied by people and conversation: "Only in this way can one nourish the other, so that the landscape may be evoked from both, before the eyes of a reader who is not free to touch the living grass of Cameirus with his own hands, or to feel the waves of sunlight beating upon the rocks of Lindos" (107).

The writer calls up the "spirit of place," using history, scene, and conversation. His objective is to evoke, not describe. This technique, one suited to Durrell's genius, is at the heart of the *Quartet*. Moments in sequences instead of designs would turn landscape into mere scenery. Landscape is wider, freer, more comprehensive than scenery: landscape is heraldic reality.

Although *Marine Venus* seems too long after the more compact perfections of *Prospero's Cell*, its extendedness is deliberate. There is more to say about Rhodes than about Corfu, and for Durrell there was time to explore and contemplate the lost cities and the vestiges of the age of the knights. The experiencing of these records of the past, these historical big moments, is tempered by the smaller pleasures of the garden of the Villa Cleobolus where he writes.

The work includes a calendar of flowers and saints, a list of peasant remedies, and a short bibliography: mumbo-jumbo and history, reason and myth. It all adds up.

III Bitter Lemons

The history of Cyprus is involved with the history of several great empires: the Persian, Roman, Byzantine, and English. A chronic trouble spot, Cyprus has belonged to many different countries as well as to itself. Durrell writes in *Bitter Lemons* of the Cyprus he knew during the years from 1953 to 1956, critical ones for Cyprus. In the *Preface* to the work he fairly states his point of view: "I went to the island as a private individual and settled in the Greek village of Bellapaix. Subsequent events as recorded in these pages are seen, whenever possible, through the eyes of my hospitable fellow-villagers, and I would like to think that this book was a not ineffective monument raised to the Cypriot peasantry and the island landscape " (9).

Durrell's Cyprus is almost as fabulous as his Alexandria—with its "echoes from forgotten moments of history" (20). This is the island Antony gave to Cleopatra. The paths of Kitchener and Rimbaud possibly crossed here: "But that is what islands are for; they are places where different destinies can meet and intersect in the full isolation of time" (20).

Bitter Lemons, combining as it does clear, leisurely writing with mature observation, may be the finest moment in Durrell's career to date for those readers who shy away from experiment. It is truly a fascinating book, and its fascination is partly a function of its irresponsibleness as a piece of literature and its complete responsibleness as a human document. In so-called travel books a happy meeting between writer and reader may come at any odd moment without guilty side-glances at the problems of formal structure.

Structurally travel books are loose. Usually there are quaint character guides, hotel keepers, and taxi drivers. Uusally there is abundant comment on costumes, customs, mores, morals, and language idiosyncrasies. There is local scenery galore, but the characters and the settings, sociological and geographical factors, need not contribute to a bigger pattern. There is always some story but no plot.

Bitter Lemons is a high level example of the kind of writing which may be too hastily judged as merely popular. True, it sells as well as it reads. It was Durrell's first hit, but it is not trivial. Its punches are effective, even decisive. By the end of *Bitter Lemons* one has been converted to the Cypriot cause in the most effective terms: one is simply pro-Cypriot. How is it done?

First of all, the writer flatters—in a courteous sort of way. Allusions are subtle enough but neither obscure nor condescending. On the very first page a reference to Stendhal glides by easily while explaining itself. Then one of those fortuitous characters always remembered (or invented) by travel-writers comes along quickly, and the ensuing conversation about Cyprus informs while it entertains. One learns that Durrell is on his way to Cyprus to *live* there—and the reader feels he, also, is *in*.

Durrell reports how he found a book about Cyprus by a Mrs. Lewis, dated 1893, in Trieste during an air raid. It was staring at him "from a jumble of fruit and books, and a whole drift of smashed second-hand discs" (21). He simply took it. Quotations from Mrs. Lewis also inform and entertain, and Durrell's book is under way.

Modestly but clearly, Durrell speaks Greek. This is reassuring to the reader and a delight to a "grave looking priest" (there is always a priest handy in travel books) but not to the customs men, who fear to lose face by speaking Greek to anyone other than peasants. Father Basil, however, invites Durrell to drink with him, and eventually finds Durrell a taxi driver—the priest's cousin. With him, Durrell begins his Cyprus adventure by plunging into a political conversation (after a prelude of surliness on the part of the taxi driver). All taxi drivers are either surly or convivial; this one is both. Taxi drivers are also philosophers, political scientists, and sources of information, and are often incredibly helpful to Durrell, who is always charming to them. One who freezes with drivers, never speaks to strange priests, and shies away or condescends to peasants gets nowhere. Durrell's manner (no smirking and no bravado) wins him friends. He is a good companion. It is not long before the island accepts and understands him just as he accepts and understands the island; and the reader, delighted with the gently intoxicating prose, cooperates fully.

The schoolmaster Panos is another one of Durrell's many guides and mentors. Panos talks much about the geography and the history of Cyprus. Cypriot conversation is generally punctuated with *ouzo* (a potent liquor), dried octopus (a local cocktail snack), and sharp analyses of "freedom." The talk is heady. Durrell also begins to introject the Levantine wisdom—"to wait and see." In time, he will find his house and his peace.

The music of a flute coming from Clito's wine store attracts him. In the store he meets the drunken Frangos whose hostility he cleverly converts into sheepishness by inventing for himself a brother martyred in the war. Clito recommends the Turk Sabri as the man to help Durrell find a house.

The buying of the house is an amusing, instructive, characteristic event. It is mixed with that delicate combination of respect for peasants and for the ability to keep, if not ahead, then at least abreast of their chicanery with tricks of one's own. The Turkish real-estate agent sends Durrell to a Greek builder, Andreas Kallergis, for the next step is to alter the house. With Kallergis he partakes of sweet jam and water. More friendliness follows. Durrell's success with neighbors and workmen is part of the sweetness and light of this book. Among the workers Mr. Honey, "the philosopher of main drainage," is memorable. As a plumber he knows where it all goes in the end!

There are also non-peasants—the straight characters and friends—like Marie, the "nereid," who is also planning to build, and friends-from-home and friends-of-friends with houses of their own on Cyprus with whom to talk English-talk, albeit exiled-English, and from whom to learn the more subtle things about Cyprus: "They brought with them fragments of history and legend to set against the village lore. . . . Through them I caught a glimpse, not only of Cyprus as she is today, but of the eternal Cyprus which had for so long attracted the attention of travellers like them" (103).

Durrell keeps a notebook which becomes "cross-hatched" with the things he is learning. He inserts a few pages of it into the text. He records a talk with Alexis, an old friend with whom he had escaped to Crete in 1941. Also, local gossip, local color, and personal anecdotes are mixed with serious matters and philosophical speculations. The result of so much "cross-hatching" is plaid-like. The work has more texture and design than structure; but it is effective.

Durrell's students, to whom he teaches English at the Nicosia Gymnasium, and their parents, with whom he lives in his village home, are all expert informants. The book is fully packed. And always as background is the "sun-bruised" island itself.

The latter part of the work is less sunny, for it has more to do with Durrell's job. The job takes him from his village home into the "Information Office," away from the sky, sea, and sun. All in all, Durrell appears as an adequate administrator—on the side of "justice" for the Cypriots. Meditative and perceptive, he is given to prophetic comments: "Paul's truth is not mine—and indeed here in Cyprus one is aware, as in no other place, that Christianity is but a brilliant mosaic of half-truths" (171). With reference to the ubiquitous talk of what-to-do-with-Cyprus-and-how-to-do-it, Durrell says: "I could not find my way forward among all these mutually contradictory propositions; it seemed to me that everybody was right and everybody wrong" (194).

But the propositions and the talk finally give way to violence—with *real* soldiers, bullets, and bombs. Durrell prepares to leave Cyprus. The parting word of wisdom comes from a taxi driver with whom Durrell was having "one of those Greek conversations which carry with them a hallucinating surrealist flavour. . . ." The driver says that, although the Cypriots love the British, the Cypriots will have to go on killing the British "with regret, even with affection" (251).

Bitter Lemons is a powerful mixture of *ouzo*, good talk, and the facts of man's procrastination and indifference. The taste is predominantly bitter.

IV Holiday *Sketches*

Durrell's recent contributions to *Holiday*, the lush, status-conscious American periodical, are typical of his talent for evoking places.[5] They are essentially ritualistic. During the liturgy a guide, a mentor, a peasant-prophet or a knight-of-the-road initiates the readers. The sacraments range from wild boar to cheese fondue.

Take an old sea captain, his daughter, a jug of wine, and a trip to Grenoble. The daughter's name is Martine; the jug is wicker-covered (twelve liter capacity). The old sea captain lurches down a hill with the jug which he asks Durrell to deliver to his daughter in Grenoble. During the trip to Grenoble, we learn something of the students, faculties, curricula, and housing conditions at the university. A student philosophizes about poets and scientists: Scientists are "poets of ideas." Then a visit *chez Dominique*, student-frequented spot, and a trip in the cablecar, with the whole city spread out beneath in lights and colors and lines, followed by the odors and tastes of food, and a peep over a high wall into Stendhal's apparently inaccessible garden. But *we* get in, admitted by a silvery lady who cannot refuse us, for we have the key to unlock secret gardens: charm and sincerity.

In Provence the guide has a map of the region tattooed on his chest (on his personal map of Provence, his navel is his hometown!), and we make friends with him because he is pleased to see us carrying a copy of the poems of Mistral. In Provence the cheeses and the wine are part of the landscape—along with the vines, cypresses, and olives which properly belong there. We talk with the tragic Count de C. J., a recluse, and time passes. Hurts are healed. The farewell dinner is vinously alliterative: "barrels, bottles, buts, and bins of wine."

Next, we go down the Rhone, *grénouilles à la creme* and *escargots*. Also fondues, onion soup, truffles, mushrooms, frog legs (in cream and sauteed), trout, duck, pheasant, thrush, quail, eels in wine, sheep's breasts, mutton, lamb, stuffed duck—and finally wild boar!

In another sketch we go directly to Avignon with a plumber called Raoul—an "infant Gargantua" (Rabelais is never far away in Durrell's writing). Raoul is to fetch his bride—called Laura, of course—from Avignon. So we go down the Rhone to Avignon, past the Pont du Gard, which the plumber admires hugely. He is a perceptive plumber, and Laura is all we could hope for.

In the next sketch a friend in the British diplomatic corps (Geneva), who knows much and explains well, guides us skillfully and smoothly through the "banker's architecture" of the Palais des Nations. He threatens with too many literary allusions so that he may appear cultured, and he overburdens with food: snails and "viande des Grisons." Calvin is repressed, and the meal ends with a "tot of rust-colored Armagnac" and with the performance of an amusing cuckoo clock.

The sketch called "In Praise of Fanatics" exalts the honesty of fulfilling one's vision. The editor of the village paper is the guide. An uneducated postman who had dreamed of a palace dedicated his life to reproducing his dream. The result is a fantastic montage of mixed elements. Yet the vision, Durrell insists, is "intact."

Another celebrated fanatic is also exalted—Chabert, the chef. The phrase "cleaned-palated" used to describe the prerequisite to savoring wine or food has a spiritual intensity as Durrell uses it. It combines reverently and joyously with his *eleventh* commandment—"Drink wine to talk well." To Durrell, reverence and joy are intimates. The dinner at Chabert's develops "like a Bach fugue."

Prosper, a "knight-of-the-road" who peddles SAVEGOOSE (a

remedy for liver complaint in geese) and who is himself suffering from liver complaint, is the guide through Gascony. The great moment is perhaps not the discovery of D'Artagnan's real birthplace (Dumas, says the knight of the road, had been quite wrong), but the discovery of a wonderful remedy for illness: arquebuse, a drink made of pure alcohol and macerated herbs by the fathers of St. Genis Laval and considered a "vulnerary." A "vulnerary" cures wounds—internally and externally. Here, then, is our remedy: drink!

A crisis is avoided when the wine to be drunk with the roasted pigeon on toast turns out to be not quite sweet but only fruity—as a good Grenache should be. No cola drinks here.

To Durrell eating and drinking are redemptive. Travel is a function of good-natured curiosity, and places and people are the warp and woof of life.

CHAPTER 9

The Plays

LIVING is like writing a book: at first the space between the covers seems infinitely expandable. But hard-bound or paper-cover, both lives and books must round off. A writer tries to use the space assigned to him wisely. The critic's work merely follows the writer's; the critic does no charting and arranges no climaxes by himself. Durrell's decision to round off the first half-century of his life with a verse drama, *An Irish Faustus* (1964), is emphatic. The work is less spectacular than earlier works but nonetheless significant.

Durrell's dramas, loosely classifiable as "verse plays," are relatively controversial items. Art is long, and life is often long enough (proverbs to the contrary) for the perfecting of at least one craft. Durrell's ability to tell a story and write a poem is not in doubt. As a dramatist, however, he has yet to convince some that he is filling his life-space wisely. Drama writing is a separate craft, and the dramatist's guild is a jealous one. Its membership is smaller and perhaps more ardent than the novelist's guild.

With Henry Miller, de Sade, and Rabelais still firing his psychic furnace, Durrell may find the combination of story, poetry, and dialogue of the verse play increasingly appropriate to his talent. In any event, Durrell has enjoyed working with his dramatic "essays." He has been more modest than critics who measure him against Racine and Corneille.[1] To date (1964) there are just three plays: *Sappho*, *Acte*, and *An Irish Faustus*. Both the production and publication histories of these works are complicated.[2] They have all been performed, in German translation, in Hamburg's Deutsches Schauspielhaus during the last several years, beginning with *Sappho* in 1959. The reviews have been less than enthusiastic but usually respectful. When *Sappho* was performed at the 1961 Edinburgh festival, it was praised as literature rather than as drama. In this study, also, the works are reviewed as literature—as attempts to *say-in-words* rather than as stage-business.

I Sappho

Although published in 1950, Durrell's first play, *Sappho,* came out of the later 1940's. It is a free and imaginative adaptation of the Sappho legend, written in equally free and imaginative verse.

The historical Sappho lived toward the end of the seventh century, B.C. She is supposed to have been in love with a handsome man named Phaon. Because he did not return her love, she leaped to her death from a high cliff—the so-called Leucadian Rock. Only fragments of the real Sappho's poetry have survived. Now her fame is largely legendary—and notorious. The persistence with which her name has been linked with homosexuality is related to her leadership of a female literary group. Ironically, the more she has been defended from the charge of immoral and abnormal behavior, the more the charges have stuck. Durrell, however, uses little of the historical or scandalous associations. Neither suicide nor abnormal sexuality is linked with his Sappho, who appears complex, thoughtful, intelligent, perceptive, and talented. For all her sensitivity, she is capable of making decisions and taking action. Her slight stammer is charming and only lightly symptomatic of inner tensions.

Durrell's Sappho is caught up in a moment of history, the war between Lesbos and Athens. This is Lesbos' moment of glory as potential center of an empire. Summer is Sappho's element, and the play symbolically opens toward the end of summer. While Lesbos awaits news of its war against Athens, Sappho awaits more personal resolutions. This may also be her moment of glory.

Durrell tells his story in nine scenes. After a prologue by Minos, the pedant, three maids appear: Chloe, Doris, and Joy. They belong to "a rich Greek family in Lesbos *circa* 650" (11). While tidying the room, they comment, chorus-like, and explain that Chloe is to marry the son of Diomedes, who lies in drunken sleep on a couch in the "spacious room." When awakened, Diomedes speaks with an Irish accent! He is a poet of sorts, a man of feeling who has won the laurel from Sappho twice in the past week. The maids carry him off stage.

Minos, Sappho's teacher, enters—also Sappho, wearing a wig of gold—"haggard and sleepy." Minos describes her as "lovely, famous and discontented" (18). Sappho has been writing a marriage song for a rival poet, Alcaeus. Sappho and Minos discuss the aptness of a metaphor which Minos finds trite. He suggests it may be redeemed by *labeling* it as trite. The suggestion signifies, for the choice appears to be between using old familiar things with due recognition of their triteness, thus soliciting the friendly cooperation of critic and reader—or continuing the constant and painful search for new metaphors, new forms, new insights. Durrell may be making a bid here for understanding. The play, the poem, or the morality—any one of the old *forms*—is redeemable only through ironic self-awareness: the labeling of itself as trite.

Minos and Sappho also talk of the imminent return of General Pittakos. They talk of Sappho's background, the generosity and permissiveness of her husband, Kreon, who has given her a "white house" of her own. They discuss the half-forgotten earthquake. It is apparent that the older men, Kreon and Minos, identify with the time *before* the quake.

The plot aspect of the work now gets under way. Exposition is handled with little attempt at subtlety. What one needs to know is told by those who know it. The conversation between Sappho and her teacher focuses on Sappho. Her origin is mysterious. After the earthquake she had been found wandering the streets—a little girl knowing only her own name. Now Sappho is concerned that she is not longing for the absent Pittakos, her former lover. Safely married to Kreon, she feels her age and is bored. She admits that she is loved, famous, idle, rich—but she is not happy.

In the next scene, Kreon, "a tall, severe-looking man," explains that he has hired a diver, Phaon, Pittakos' twin brother, who is said to be mad, to recover old records from the submerged city. Sappho opposes the diving, but Kreon reminds her that the oracle recommended the search. Twice Minos remarks: "Everyone has the right to ruin his life" (30, 33).

Minos reminds Sappho, after Kreon departs, that she loved Pittakos. Sappho sighs. She has never been satisfied:

> All women dream they will become
> One man's lieutenant, critic and admirer,
> And the same man's lover and accomplice.

Either I was greedy or the qualities
Have never met within a single skin.   (36)

Sappho steps out of the fiction, finds that love is not what the
poet has said, and her ironic self-consciousness adds another dimension to the play. In their critical soliloquies, Minos and Sappho are each given a second voice—a voice in brackets. This "dual
voice" checks the conscience of the first. And Sappho as the voice
of the oracle has still a third voice. These devices are not subtle,
but they do their work adequately.

The story is properly predictable from the premises and prom-
ises, and it unfolds as it must. Sappho receives a present from
Pittakos, a gold bracelet still clasping the former owner's severed
arm. Then Phaon enters. He is urged to speak, becomes impertinent, apologizes. Sappho and Phaon quickly find their areas of
alikeness. Phaon says: "My life has become a posthumous one"
(47). Sappho understands and identifies with Phaon's lostness.
Phaon has had leprosy, and he sees time as "a contemptible re-
fracting medium" (51). Then Sappho asks an important question:

Tell me something: did you lose at last
That sense of limitless complaint against yourself,
Or did you never feel it like those others
Who move upon the surface of normal discontents,
Scratched small by talk or envy of their neighbors
D-do you understand me?   (51)

It is Phaon's turn to understand. After more talk, he echoes
Minos: "Everyone has the right to ruin his life" (54). And at this
moment, when Phaon and Sappho seem to find each other, Minos
announces: "I am that I am" (54). Sappho, as if addressing an
obstinate God, good-naturedly objects: "We can put up with that.
It is your self-content/ That makes you odious in what you seem"
(55).

Minos is to be of no help. He will choose his security over his
affection for his old pupil. Sappho and Phaon turn their backs on
such complacency. Minos is the teacher of children, the God-
figure that one outgrows. But Phaon knows the *way:*

Deliberately, by patience to eliminate
Within ourselves, the medium of ourselves,
What is not freedom, leaving us what is.   (55)

Minos says: "Ach! All this abstract talk has made me dizzy" (58).

A contest follows. Epigrams on "Freedom" are composed by Diomedes, Minos, Sappho. The scene dissolves. Sappho and Phaon, alone, further explore their affinity. Phaon reads Sappho's palm. In a love-duet, they search the counterpoint and transcendence of love. They embrace. Their love-night begins. *Together* they say the lines that try to say the unsayable:

> Damned in effect and still neglecting cause,
> Soft brief and awkward as the kisses which combine
> To intersect with death till time follows us, time
> Finds and detains us here in time,
> In this eternal pause,
> Fumbling outside immortality's immobile doors.   (78)

Later Kreon comes for Sappho and takes her home. At this time Minos announces that Diomedes' son has died in battle. Meanwhile Kreon is delighted with his tablets which Phaon has fetched for him from the sea. Phaon now wants to go back to his island.

Athens has fallen. Pittakos returns victorious. He has stated his terms. He believes in the "superior law and order" of Lesbos, in "freedom," and in the other abstractions of the demagogue and of the righteous conqueror. There is talk of empire and of Pittakos as tyrant. So Pittakos modestly decides to seek the oracle's advice. But first Pittakos and Sappho talk together. Pittakos is a believer; Sappho has reason to be skeptical: "I think the oracle is simply an old woman," she says (127). Pittakos is shocked. Sappho advises him to give up his ambitions: "Seals, dignities, titles, offices, everything" (129). Pittakos replies: "I cannot colonize ideas. My theatre is this world" (130).

The issue is now clear and the end is in sight. Pittakos belittles Sappho's morality and belief in free will. Sword and stylus are both delusions. He is a man of action, and as such disparages metaphors and moralities. He tells Sappho *he* killed Diomedes' son because he was a coward. Pittakos' defense is destiny: "Our fault lies in conditions given us . . ." (140). Sappho tries to kill him when he dares her to act as a moral being, but he fends off the blow.

Diomedes takes poison and dies. Sappho confesses to the dying man that she is the voice of the masked oracle. Kreon, thinking that he has inadvertently married his own daughter, a conclusion wrongly deduced from the rescued tablets, goes to the oracle for advice. So does Pittakos. Sappho as the voice of the oracle tells Kreon that his fate is not to know. He must undergo the punishments prescribed by law.

Pittakos becomes tyrant. Sappho and Kreon are exiled to Corinth, but Pittakos holds Sappho's children as hostages. Kreon dies. When Sappho later learns that her son has been killed accidentally, she blames Pittakos, works against his interests in Corinth, and at the end of fifteen years returns to Lesbos.

Pittakos and Phaon (the defeated Pittakos has sought refuge with his brother) are both killed. Sappho is now free—if her "icy indifference" can be called freedom:

> Everyone is afraid of me.
> All that I could not solicit of love,
> I gained at last in fear. I am strong
> In fear now, not in love.
> It has a different taste but it fills the space.   (185-86)

Her last words are "Weep, Weep, Weep" (186).

Henry Miller was enthusiastic about *Sappho*. He compared it to Shakespeare ". . . with a tincture of Eliot's gray foreboding wisdom." Durrell had sent Miller the proofs (in 1950) with a characteristic postscript: "A bit turgid but there are good things in it." [3] Durrell's judgment is fairer than Miller's; it is less enthusiastic but somehow more stimulating. The "good things" in *Sappho* are so good that back in 1950, before the *Quartet* destroyed Durrell's anonymity once and for all, this verse play carried its relative obscurity with dignity. It is essentially a quiet work, not designed for revolution or hyperbole—and unsuitable to the stage. (So are Shakespeare and T. S. Eliot.) It moves *toward* high values, and its failure as drama is gently reassuring. It can be performed—and has been—on radio and at festivals where literary and *esthetico-philosophico* values (essentially auditory and oral experiences) are of the essence. *Sappho* is literature.

II Acte

Durrell counts his second verse play, *Acte*, as his first drama, because it was the first one he wrote for the stage as such.[4] Like

Sappho, it is an adaptation of history. The Roman Emperor Nero is supposed to have had a favorite slave-concubine named Acte. Loving her dearly—or pretending to love her—Nero fantasied that she was of royal birth, the daughter of a king; some say he even planned to marry her. Durrell's Acte is a princess, daughter of King Corvinus of Scythia; and Nero's love for her is casual and childlike. She makes him soup, and they eat and talk together in one of the enormous kitchens of the palace. Although at one time she contemplates murdering him, the relationship is low pitched.

A clever man by the name of Gaius (or Titus) Petronius is supposed to have lived at Nero's court as a privileged companion of the corrupt Nero. Inventor and director of palace pleasures, he passed judgment on Nero's plans for fun (*elegantiae arbiter*). His fame as the author of the *Satyricon* is based on a combination of merit and scandal. His death as a suicide was a pleasant social event.

The historical Petronius has been called wanton, cynical, and corrupt. Durrell's Petronius Arbiter, an enormous man with enormous fists, seems less wanton than wise, less cynical and corrupt than sophisticated. He is not introduced into the drama until the third act. At once he becomes the spokesman for the theory which backs the action—and the director of the plot-finale as well as the author of the plot-within-the-plot which inaccurately predicts reality.

As arbiter of taste, Petronius ultimately convinces Nero to give the two star-crossed lovers, Acte and the Roman general Fabius, "freedom" in which to destroy each other—a refined punishment. Life and art, the real and the image, are confounded in the play's dramatic moment of truth in which drama dwindles to indifferent anticlimax.

Obviously *Acte* is no ordinary Broadway or West End commercial success. The "classical" dramas of Greece and France, and the meditative poetry-dialogues of T. S. Eliot predict this kind of drama; and, as in them, the conflicts are kept neat and honest—to the point of ingenuousness.

It is a talky play. In the beginning, it tells much of what is coming; and, when it ends, it tells what came. At times the absence of clichés and dramatic platitudes is as startling as their presence at other times.[5] The action moves steadily toward the grayness of the ending. The final mood is all-passion-and-irony-spent.

The "plot" is complicated. During the reign of Nero, Scythia has been occupied by Rome for twenty years. It is presently ruled by the cruel satrap Metellus. A recent revolt has been subdued by the Roman general Fabius, whose arrival in Scythia, however, is too late to prevent severe retaliations against the Scythians, including the blinding of Princess Acte, daughter of King Corvinus. Acte's intended husband, the brave Amar, has taken to the hills. There he plans counter-retaliations. The situation is explained in a conversation between Fabius and Metellus. They agree that Fabius is to take Acte and her old counsellor, Galba, to Rome as hostages guaranteeing peace in Scythia. Acte is discussed and her patriotism, her ardor, and her beauty are noted. Metellus doubts she is a virgin. Fabius' responses indicate more than casual interest in Acte.

The next scene shows Acte in action—bitter, determined. Her father, with paternal ambivalence, scolds and cherishes her. She shows her father that the "operation" on her eyes has not impaired their beauty, only their usefulness. Acte insists, despite the failure of three uprisings in ten years, that Scythia must still be free. Her concern with freedom is a kind of psychic blindness. She plans to work for Scythia in Rome, where she is confident the Romans will treat her with respect.

The next scene, night in the woods, brings Acte and Fabius together. They are alone and en route to Rome. The scene is improbable but dramatic. Fabius speaks Acte's language and knows the Scythian literature, for as a lad he lived at the Scythian court when his uncle was satrap. Fabius tells her he has chosen to avoid the villages so that the farmers will not see what has happened to their princess. Acte is skeptical. These are strange words and feelings for a Roman. Fabius' delay in reaching Scythia, he explains, was due to his visit to the tomb of Semiramis, Acte's ancestress. He loves Scythia.

Fabius and Acte disagree on Scythia's chances for freedom and on Rome's contribution to Scythian welfare. The conversation is political as well as subtly passionate. Fabius declares his devotion. Acte defends Amar, her betrothed. Duty dictates, however, that Fabius go to Gaul. Acte will go to Rome, where Fabius hopes she may regain her sight. Suddenly she tries to kill Fabius with his own dagger, which he has handed to her while investigating a disturbance in the woods. He disarms her easily. Then Acte tells him that she had been raped by her sister's husband. *Now* she is all Scythian—not a woman, not a prisoner, not a princess: "Take heed!" They part.

The scene that follows was not performed in Hamburg. It contains an exchange, in the woods, of verbal amenities and hostilities between Amar and Fabius. Amar asserts Fabius' essential Scythian identification, even to a blood-brother relationship, ring and all. Fabius answers: "I am a Roman." Amar finds Fabius incorruptible. Acte will perhaps also find him incorruptible, for patriotism and love are both traditionally incorruptible. The pressure has been building in Fabius: Acte or Rome!

The first act ends with a scene between Acte and Fabius in a room on the Via Appia, not far from Rome—in which Fabius and Acte embrace: "I hate you, Roman," says Acte, in his arms. She has found Rome cold, the whole world cold—without Fabius. They become lovers.

The second act furthers the complications. Acte's correspondence with Fabius, who is now in Gaul, is indiscreet, even dangerous; but love runs true to its traditional derring-do. Acte has regained partial sight. She can now distinguish light and shadow. In an interlude scene, Fabius and Acte make love. They are *both* prisoners—of love. Acte's adviser, Galba, articulates his apprehensions. No good will come of this. The tension grows. Acte, in her love for Fabius, fantasies a coup in which Fabius would come to power in Rome and rule *with his wife Flavia.* Acte believes she has only two concerns—Fabius' good and Scythia's good. Her psychological innocence (combined with her physiological blindness) begins to reach tragic proportions of willfulness and rationalization. She will fail.

A highly imaginative scene with Nero follows. For some time Acte has been *rendezvousing* with Nero in one of the great, abandoned kitchens of the palace. There Acte cooks simple things for Nero, talks with him, and mothers him; she *could* also assassinate him. Galba, Acte's adviser, observes one of these scenes between Acte and Nero. Nero's madness (he is both animal and god) is logical and frightening. His symptoms are clinically valid and artistically compelling. The ghost of his mother conveniently appears near the end of the rendezvous scene, and he follows the ghost off stage. Galba warns Acte to take care. Galba blows out the candles, and he and Acte exit quickly.

The encounter, predictable (and dramatically correct) between Fabius' wife, Flavia, and Acte follows immediately. Acte gives audience to her lover's mate who is regal, bitter, direct. She hates Fabius, but she submits to the passion which her coldness perversely arouses in him. "I have a heart," Acte says. Flavia's, however, has turned to stone. She jeers at Acte's commitment to duty, and proceeds to destroy Acte's image of Fabius. He has sent Flavia to Acte to plead for the return of his incriminating letters to her, for Nero suspects Fabius of treason.

The scene between Flavia and Acte is full of dramatic variables: duty versus love versus passion versus expediency. Acte, a woman of feeling and commitment confronts Flavia, the cynical sophisticate. The facts are on Flavia's side. Fabius has feared for his life. Acte has truly felt that she was motivated to do good, to save her country, to save her lover—and his wife and child. Flavia's skepticism is a function of experience. Acte's heartbreak is poignantly innocent. Galba has betrayed Acte to Flavia and Flavia's uncle, Petronius Arbiter, whose influence over Nero is strong and calculated. Acte must not go to Nero and tell all—as her impulse suggests. Only Petronius can save them, Flavia argues.

There is room, esthetically as well as physically, for one more big scene between Acte and Fabius. But first Petronius Arbiter convinces Nero to release both Fabius and Acte, who have been arrested, and to let "life" punish them. Nero's interest in Petronius' scheme is both fiendish and childlike. Petronius will write the *story* of Acte and Fabius, and Nero will author *reality*. Petronius convinces Nero that artistic writers do not kill off their characters. The artist must be an observer. Life itself will provide the resolution—and, if Nero releases Acte and Fabius, they will most probably destroy one another, thus expiating their sins. They will create their own punishments.

The end has been implicit in the beginning. Acte has wanted too much. Her patriotism is as impatient as her passion; and, after she is allowed to "escape" she plans a great rebellion. She hopes to destroy the Roman conquerors. In a house in Brindisi, on her way home, she encounters Fabius for the last time. He has orders to march on Scythia, to quell the rebellion—and the rebel princess. The scene is fulfilling, for Acte and Fabius are now informed by "life"; Acte has no reason to trust Fabius, and Fabius has no reason to postpone his duty. They speak of destiny and history, the plans and the patterns of life. Fabius has thought of a love-death pact with Acte. Also, he is willing to send her to Egypt for sanctuary. Acte's refusal to die or flee with Fabius is the last word of a queen. The heartache will stay, but now her patriotism integrates her. She is ready to die—as queen. And she does.

Later, in the final scene of the drama, Petronius Arbiter, who is slowly bleeding to death of wounds inflicted at his bidding by a barber, talks with his niece, Flavia. The interest shifts now almost entirely to Petronius Arbiter. Suicide is the answer to age, for suicide is under one's own control. Flavia reports to Petronius that her husband has become a drunkard after his victory over Scythia —he has beheaded Acte and brought her back to Rome—and that their son has lost his mind. But Arbiter is more interested in his own artificed ending of the story of Acte and Fabius. As *he* wrote the story, they run off together to live—not happily, but in love— in Egypt.

Petronius Arbiter has the last word. His advice to Flavia is too late for her, but in time for the audience: "You must say *yes* to life." Strange advice from a suicide to a bitter, enlightened Roman lady! But then this is a strange play as it investigates life, love, duty, and other ultimates. Yet Acte is memorable. Arbiter is memorable. And the impact is real.

III   An Irish Faustus

Durrell's most recently (1964) published work is another verse play—a "morality" in nine scenes. It opens in the library of Queen Katherine's palace in Galway, Ireland. Faustus, "tall and grave and dressed in black," is instructing the young Margaret, the queen's beautiful niece, in science and magic. Faustus and Margaret discuss the limitations of science. Margaret is a good student. Faustus' notions, she says, "mock Aristotle" in that they are not completely functions of reason. Faustus is delighted with Margaret's perceptivity. Margaret asks, "The desire to prove is a sort of death, then?" "Yes," says Faustus, but this desire to prove is also an obligation: "We are both bound to it and yet bound to try to surmount it" (9). Margaret's response is simple but precise: "A wearisome chain." Margaret quickly asks to be taught "vision," and Faustus defines the paradox. He can teach nothing she does not already know. His devices and metaphors are "initiatory not didactic" (9-10).

Margaret closes the book she is holding and admits for the first time that she sees—"but very dimly." Faustus' enthusiasm is not easily subdued. He exclaims:

> To domesticate magic, that is science;
> To accept the limitations of scientific rule,
> That is magic, or leads to magic.   (10)

Margaret calls it a trick, yet she now understands more than she realizes perhaps, for her response includes the sophisticated concept of "refining by negatives." The final "field of grace" is a function of "dreaming" (10).

This talk itself suggests something more than the *there-must-be-something-more-than-science* of religious sentimentalism. What follows is a fable and a fairy tale, a story shadowed onstage with words and rituals, containing a ring made of transmuted gold which itself possesses the frightening power to transmute anything the possessor of the ring wishes to transmute. But the story is not *about* the ring. It *contains* the ring.

The play is "domesticated," full of talk, and as much about itself as it is about the gold. It is full of props and trappings: a cross, a ring, a stake (to fix the vampire once and for all), and improbable characters like the vampire, Eric the Red; the traditional good-humored Mephisto, Faustus' double; a rascally pardoner, honest in his depravity; and Matthew the Hermit (from Big Sur, perhaps) who works at doing nothing. And when in the last scene Martin, Matthew, Mephisto, and Faustus sit down to a game of cards, the "light slowly fades turning them into silhouettes. . . ." (91). They are fragile characters.

By the end of the first scene Queen Katherine has blackmailed Margaret into helping her steal the ring and the instructions for using it. When the queen threatens to have Margaret's mother's

body dug up and as a suicide thrown to the dogs, Margaret cooperates. Katherine then gently reassures Margaret: "No harm will
come of it, you will see" (17).

The scene shifts to the marketplace, where Martin, "a big fat
man with a distinctly comic turn of speech," is selling pardons. He
and his cadaverous assistant are comic characters. Faustus enters.
Their conversation deals with Martin's pains and troubles. Matthew the Hermit is a near neighbor of Martin's, and Martin has a
letter for Faustus from Matthew. The report is that Matthew is
happy. He and Martin play cards evenings. Martin offers to sell
Faustus, too, a pardon: "You must have done something," he says.
"And everything is a sin for somebody." But Martin has no pardon
for "intellectual pride" (24). He has nothing for Faustus.

Mephisto appears in the cabinet of Faustus, which is outfitted
with alchemist's devices. Appropriately, Mephisto is Faustus' approximate double. He appears after Faustus has been staring into
the mirror. Mephisto, who has a "soft mordant voice," is sophisticated and poised. He has come about the ring. As to his probability, he remarks reasonably: "Well, after all, if I did not exist it
might be . . . / Necessary to invent me" (32). Mephisto tells
Faustus that Queen Katharine has the ring. It was Eric the Red,
the queen's late husband, who had originally ordered the ring to
be made by Tremethius, the magician, with whom both Matthew
and Faustus had studied. Tremethius had followed the black arts;
Faustus, the white. Tremethius was threatened with death unless
he made the ring, Faustus explains. Mephisto replies: "There will
always be excuses to be made for folly" (33).

Tremethius was executed by Eric, and Eric vanished. Faustus
found the ring together with a letter telling him to hide the ring.
Faustus' explanations to Mephisto are ingenuous. At once Mephisto focuses the issue: "You should have either tried to destroy
it or . . ./ To use it man; one or the other, one or the other" (35).

Faustus' subsequent attempts to destroy the ring, his banish-
ment as reward for "saving" his queen from madness, and the
quiet ending in the game of cards with Faustus, Mephisto, Martin, and Matthew are easily unfolded in the ensuing scenes. The
work is a "morality in nine scenes" and not a *drama*—and it carries its responsibility to tell a story with simple dignity.

These characters do not need to be more than well-cut silhouettes. The stage business is concisely contrived. The ring, which Faustus has stored in a strongbox, is easily stolen. The characters are also props and devices. Accepting them as such allows the "play" to move through its cadences to its quiet, understated resolution.

Faustus goes back to the origin of things, with a piece of the true cross (counterfeited by Martin) loaned to him by Anselm, the clergyman, in order to destroy the gold ring once and for all. The cross burns, but then so does the ring; and Faustus is content to have destroyed the transmuted stuff. Mephisto has urged him to use it, to take up the challenge for power, but he decides to take action *backward* and undo what is done.

Both Martin and Mephisto say that, if they had not existed, man would have had to invent them. Katherine, cured of her sickness, deprived of her vampire husband and the ring, acknowledges her debt to Faustus and then banishes him. Margaret, too, dwindles to nothing in this "initiatory" version of the old Faustus story.

The trouble may be that this work is too artfully simple and ingenuously contrived for a pre-judged Durrell to have created—and so it must be a mistake. As a piece of didacticism, not as initiation and ritual, it has been translated into "meaning." The result of this kind of explication is first disarming, then alarming. One cannot get the vision unless the potential is already there. The paradox of this curious work is that its *meaning* is almost pure vision, and it ought to work on stage *despite*—that is, through negatives—not *because*.

The limitations of the stage are definitive. Like science, the stage tends to domesticate magic. Equating the imponderables of nuclear energy with an alchemist's dilemma is a daring regression. Such a play seems to speak directly to children. Its trappings and tricks are basic. Besides, children ask to be initiated rather than instructed; and so the funny professor, the vampire, the queen, the bad men, and the magic ring are adequate. Anyway, *An Irish Faustus* is half-way out of the theater and on its way to the cinema. Cinematic imperatives restore magic to its proper glory. It is not surprising that Durrell has become seriously interested in "movies." [6] Many "artists" have lately been testing the limits of this still comparatively new merger between literature and pictures that move, and the best directors have turned away from merely photographing stage plays. Although creating for the commercial cinema is supposed to be frustrating for the ordinary novelist, the experimenter in Durrell (as well as the painter and poet) may spark in this medium.

CHAPTER 10

Lawrence Durrell: Place and Rank

A SUMMING up is now in order. Neatness is well served by drawing a line under a set of events and adding them up to find a total which may then be evaluated. The many items in the Durrell canon are not easily totaled, however, for they range widely in form and function. Nevertheless, many judgments have now been passed on almost everything that Durrell has written. The enthusiasts have abused superlatives so that the more moderate evaluators have over-corrected and understated. But few completely hostile voices have been raised; for among the many words Durrell has patterned into prose, poetry, and his own version of "heightened speech"—there are some to please every taste.[1]

The critical evaluations become more precise as they relate themselves to specific categories of Durrell's work—to his poetry, to his critical ideas, to his travel writing, to his humorous sketches, to his early novels, or to his *Quartet*—along any one (or all) of a number of possible dimensions such as rhetoric and meaning. And the critical judgments which try to *place* the object before *ranking* it are the most clearly defined of all. The ornithologist's standard of measurement—a bird is larger or smaller than a robin—requires only knowledge of the size of a robin and the ability to identify the other creatures as birds. Literature poses a more difficult case. Although no attempt will be made to place and rank *all* aspects of Durrell's production, some summary statements can now safely be made about the directions such judgments have been taking. The criterion "robin," however, is problematic.

I *Place*

"Place" refers to *what, when,* and *where,* as in the statement: "If I could only *place* him I could deal with him." When a critic labels a writer as an Elizabethan poet, a contemporary French anti-novelist, or a nineteenth-century American regionalist, the critic is placing the writer. If one could only *place* Durrell, one could deal with him.

Simplifying, one can say that as a poet Durrell is "related" to W. H. Auden, Robert Graves, and T. S. Eliot. He is in a tradition. However, Durrell's own poetry is bawdy, robust, and lyrical by turns. Again and again his poems are not quite pure Auden, pure Graves, or pure Eliot. Yet there is little difficulty in *placing* the poetry, for it has neither broken containers nor destroyed forms despite Durrell's subtle experiments with unusual word combinations.

As a critic, Durrell is both perceptive and honest; but his few critical pieces interpret what he is interested in and what he is doing rather than reveal new truths. His concept of "heraldic reality" is a personal insight, and as such it illuminates his own work more than the writings of others. As a writer of travel articles and books, he has improved the medium but not transcended it. As a humorist, he has been called "pure Wodehouse." As a dramatist, he is confessedly provisional—and even his admirers sometimes see him "merely as a poet" who loves the theater.

Not really difficult to place as poet, critic, travel writer, humorist, and dramatist (except that he is *all* of these things), Durrell as a novelist is easily misplaced. When imaginative critics first saw that Joyce's *Ulysses* could not be evaluated fairly in any of the traditional categories of novels, they created a new class for "books-like-*Ulysses.*" *Ulysses* is now ranked as still the best in that class. And the class of novels which could be called "books-like-*Finnegans Wake*" has only one entry to date. Is the *Quartet* a class-making novel? Is it the first entry in a new class to be called "books-like-the *Quartet?*"

Durrell's *early* novels can be variously placed as something-like-Henry Miller, something-like-Aldous Huxley, something-like-Norman Douglas, for example; and they have been so described (Chapter 3 of this study). But *The Alexandria Quartet* is pleasantly recalcitrant. If the Durrell of the *Quartet* is placed as primarily a traditional poet writing perfervid prose rather than as a serious, contemporary, experimental novelist, then the *Quartet* tends to become an exotic epic, with touches of magical lyricism at the best, and eczematic patches of purple writing at the worst.

Furthermore, one must remember that Durrell is often an ironist. As his Petronius in *Acte* says: "There is only ironic truth, no other variety." [2] Extreme caution is necessary lest a contemporary *Satyricon* be misplaced as a romantic historical novel or as a pretentious experiment.

Attempts to place Durrell as a "modern Elizabethan" have resulted in his becoming Shakespeare's rival—and losing the contest. This kind of hyperbole usually involves the *Quartet* only. Fine ratings have been given much of the poetry, and the travel books have won high praise, particularly *Bitter Lemons*. And there are lovers of Durrell's humor who laugh aloud regularly wherever they should as they turn the pages; yet only the big four-decker has thoroughly whetted critical appetites for a rousing fight over rank. Durrell himself has confused the issues even more by denying his identification with contemporary experimentalists. Among the many things he has said to many interviewers, the following staement is noteworthy: "The trouble with modern literature . . . is that it has all gone up into the head. You give a man a thousand pages of Joyce to plow through, and what have you got? A dense jungle of egomania and forced intellectualism. What I wanted to do was to get back to the origins, reverse the trend. Modern literature goes from Rabelais to Sade. I want to get it back to Rabelais—out of the mind and back into the belly, where we can stitch it up again." [3]

This declaration certainly sounds like a rejection of both Bloom and Bloomsbury. If the repudiation of one's own time is the true mark of a modern, Durrell is properly placed as an independent modern. He is the kind of anachronism that is paradoxically quite contemporary. His romanticism is based on Freud, Jung, and Groddeck, while his major metaphor has combined mysticism with space-time concepts along his own special continuum. He has enthusiastically acknowledged both Henry Miller and T. S. Eliot as masters while revising their widely differing orthodoxies into his own vision of truth.

II *Rank*

The sum of Durrell's writings is of course heavily weighted by *The Alexandria Quartet,* and it takes precedence over the other works in attracting attention, both favorable and unfavorable.

The poetry comes second—except to a few fastidious critics who see poetry in everything of any value that Durrell has written and refuse to consider him in any other category. The travel books are preferred by some, but their qualities can be broken down into poetry and story and so resolved into the other two aspects.

Two opinions of Durrell-as-poet indicate the range of ratings he has received in this role. One reviewer wrote: "I don't actually like Durrell's poetry. It is obviously a considerable *oeuvre,* but it reminds me of some vast Hindu frieze, replete with innumerable details of pose and gesture, each of which obviously had for the artist an intense and exact significance, probably sexual, but is meaningless to the modern tourist." [4] No responsible critic has said anything worse about the poetry, and most have ranked Durrell as poet very high—as nearly "up" with Dylan Thomas. His poetry has been accepted as complementary to his prose: "Durrell's poetry and prose are like opposite sides of the same coin—all of a piece. Here are traceable the same influences (Greek, Egyptian, French), the same themes (primarily nature, love, and sex), the same preoccupation with time . . . These more than 150 poems are rich in imagery and rhythms, sensuous, polished, and brilliant." [5]

Space allows only a sampling of the range of opinion—some irresponsible, some intent on placing the work properly—that followed the appearance of the volumes of the *Quartet* between 1957 and 1960. In 1959, after the publication of *Mountolive,* a reviewer wrote: "The temptation to say merely that Durrell sometimes writes extremely well and sometimes not so well, and let it go at that, is almost, but not quite, overwhelming." After placing Durrell "on a modest scale . . . in the line of Thackeray, Stendhal, and Turgenev," the reviewer ranked Durrell comparatively high: "There is magnificence in these books, of design, of writing, and of imagination. There is something in them for almost every taste. With them, Durrell has become one of the half-dozen or so most interesting novelists writing in English." [6]

Measuring Durrell against Samuel Beckett as the "criterion robin," Gerald Sykes cast his vote for Durrell's warmth instead of Beckett's "ice." Sykes is one of the critics who ranked the fourth volume of the tetralogy very high, although he realized the difficulty of placing it: "The tetralogy ends on this note: a massive, concrete, felt statement of faith. Its calm refusal to run out of breath makes it seem almost a work of the nineteenth century. Its mood, as it nears its conclusion, is one of almost anachronistic serenity." [7]

Martin Green's report is more subtle. Self-styled as a "minority report," it is harder on Middle-Western Americans than it is on Durrell: ". . . Britain is hungry for the artist who will give *her* a world of mythical size, color, and complexity, which yet needn't be taken seriously. Durrell satisfies that hunger, however meretriciously. The American enthusiasm for him is more simple: a graduate-school vision of sin and subtlety in exotic old Alexandria, where you can forget you grew up in Ohio." [8] One more minority report balances the sample: "The possibility that his work as a whole should be thought of as a long anti-novel, a purposeful or Dadaist mingling of styles, indicates the range of its potential interest—but the possibility is undercut by the absence of the note of amused self-awareness that lends authority to such productions. At their best his ideas *are* ideas, but since they are available elsewhere and since in his preachment of them Durrell is frequently hysterical, he does not qualify as an original or subtle mind." [9]

Durrell's own claims for his work have been modest enough to disarm most hostility, and the main point at issue concerns the extent to which the *Quartet* is truly experimental. That concern is best dealt with in terms of specifics such as those outlined in chapters 5 and 6 above. Certainly Durrell has not seriously tried to top either Joyce's or Proust's deep research into the springs of memory. Nor has he probably seen himself as the only or ultimate geographer of space-time. Durrell's prose or poetry, even when the two are confounded (*delightfully* confounded, some think), always makes sense. Syntactically—from word to word—it is traditional writing. It exploits the reader's curiosity but does not betray the reader's expectations. Durrell does his share of tricks with words, but they are the honest ones of the trade. Durrell is a professional writer.

The popularity of the *Quartet* has disturbed those who distrust commercial success, but by and large both friends and critics have applauded the good taste of the book clubs rather than disparaged Durrell. Durrell has been willing to sell what he writes, and the feedback effect of selling is perhaps significant; for, if no one buys the product, the producer tends to stop producing. In the past, however, Durrell's creative activities have involved significant risks to his financial security, and his lucky hits have so far been all to the good. The future may or may not reveal the positive or negative effects of increased security. Such conjecture, especially when it is only conjecture, is impertinent.

Now let Durrell have the last words here. Only a few years ago he said: "I find art easy. I find life difficult." [10]

Notes and References

Chapter One

1. *Lawrence Durrell and Henry Miller: A Private Correspondence,* ed. George Wickes (New York, 1963), p. 328. This important collection of letters is referred to here as *A Private Correspondence.*

2. Durrell's concept of "heraldic reality" is discussed in Chapter Two below.

3. Durrell is always courteous to interviewers but not always deadly serious. In 1960 he told a reporter that he "admired" such people as Henry VIII, Villon, Sugar Ray Robinson, Anquetil, René Char, Jean Gabin, Picasso, Bonnard, Juliette Gréco, and Brassens. "Lawrence Durrell Vous Parle," *Réalitiés* (No. 178: 1960), pp. 118-19. In 1959 he indicated that he was "most in sympathy" with the following "modern writers": Montherlant, Proust, Henry Miller, Kazanzakis, Borghes, and Svevo. "Lawrence Durrell Answers a Few Questions," *Two Cities* (April 15, 1959), pp. 25-28. (Ask silly questions and you get silly—or clever—answers.)

4. *My Friend Lawrence Durrell* (Northwood, Middlesex: 1961), p. 22. This "intimate memoir" is brief, sincere, even ardent, yet Perlès feels the novel has expired with the *Quartet.*

5. *A Private Correspondence,* p. 59.

6. Gerald Durrell, *My Family and Other Animals* (New York, 1957). Gerald Durrell is a naturalist and himself a successful writer. He credits "Larry" with the suggestion that the family move to Corfu: ". . . Larry was designed by Providence to go through life like a small, blond firework, exploding ideas in other people's minds, and then curling up with catlike unctuousness and refusing to take any blame for the consequences" (p. 3).

7. See the Grove Press editions of Miller's novels formerly banned in the United States.

8. *My Friend Lawrence Durrell,* p. 11.

9. Copies of the magazines may be seen at The Houghton Library, Harvard University. The articles by Durrell, Miller, and their friends

are a good cut above college humor but well aware of their derring-do. For *The Booster* Durrell writes a sports column as Charles Norden. Alfred Perlès writes: "We have a unique literary review. . . . We sit in easy chairs drinking gin rickeys, we play golf, we listen to Bach, and we paint water colours. . . ." *The Booster* (Oct., 1937). Even the eleven-year-old Gerald Durrell contributes.

10. New York: n.d. Miller's passing references to Durrell are only part of the interest in this vibrant work.

11. Compare Father Nicholas: "What more does a man want than an olive tree, a native island, and [a] woman from his own place?" *Prospero's Cell* (New York, 1962), p. 19. Durrell adds the typewriter!

12. "Studies in Genius, VI: Groddeck," *Horizon*, XVII (June, 1948), pp. 384-403.

13. Nigel Dennis, "New Four-Star King of Novelists," *Life* (Nov. 21, 1960), pp. 96-109.

14. Dennis, p. 106.

Chapter Two

1. *A Key to Modern British Poetry* (Norman, Oklahoma, 1952), p. x. There is also a British edition: *Key to Modern Poetry* (London, 1952). All references here are to the American edition.

2. For Durrell's interest in the relatively obscure psychologist, Groddeck, see his article in *Horizon*, cited above: Chapter One, note 12.

3. *Personal Landscape: an Anthology of Exile* (London, 1945), p. 73. This is an anthology of sketches and poems by war-time "exiles" —selected from earlier issues of the magazine, *Personal Landscape*. Durrell's contributions include poems and essays. See also *A Private Correspondence*, pp. 202-3.

4. *Clea* (New York, 1960), p. 153. *Clea* is the fourth volume of Durrell's tetralogy, *The Alexandria Quartet*. In this study all references hereafter are to the Dutton Paperback edition (New York, 1961) of the four separate volumes (See "Selected Bibliography" below). Page references in the text of this study are preceded by *J* for *Justine*, *B* for *Balthazar*, *M* for *Mountolive*, and *C* for *Clea*. A later one volume edition of *The Alexandria Quartet* (New York, 1962) corrects "a number of small slips" and adds "some small passages" (Author's "Preface"). This study, however, deals with the *Quartet* as a series of four volumes, and for the convenience of American readers refers to the easily available editions of the individual volumes as noted above.

5. Durrell has no patience with those who confine truth-seeking to scientific methods. In his "Introduction" to Arthur Guirdham's *Christ*

and Freud (New York, 1962) Durrell wrote: "The highest wisdom of the world has never been presented in a form palatable to the exponents of the scientific method as we understand it" (p. 10).

6. *Collected Poems* (New York, 1960). This collection is comprehensive. Arranged by Durrell himself it includes all poems of any consequence from earlier collections. Durrell's poetry has been appearing for years in periodicals, newspapers, collections, special editions, and anthologies. A checklist of Durrell's publications (see "*Selected Bibliography*" below) that purports to be definitive has to sort out numerous reprintings and casual appearances of the several poems. For the purposes of this study this fine collection is adequate and convenient.

7. One of the joys of reading the *Quartet* is discovering Cavafy. See *The Complete Poems of Cavafy*, trans. by Rae Dalven (New York, 1961).

8. The poem "Deus Loci" has been given the special emphasis by the poet of being placed last in at least three collections in which it has appeared.

9. Probably by actual count "mirrors" dominate the imagery in the *Quartet*. See discussion below in Chapter Six.

10. In the "Author's Note" in one of the many anthologies in which Durrell's poems have been reprinted, Durrell, referring to his use of the names "Conon" and "Melissa" in his poetry, writes: "Conon is an imaginary Greek philosopher who visited me twice in my dreams, and with whom I occasionally identify myself; he is one of my masks, Melissa is another; I want my total poetic work to add up as a kind of tapestry of people, some real, some imaginary. Conon is real." Kimon Friar and John Malcolm Brinnin, eds., *Modern Poetry: American and British* (New York, 1951), p. 458.

11. *Writers at Work: the Paris Review Interviews* (Second Series, New York, 1963), p. 267. The interview took place in 1959.

12. *Ibid.*, p. 270 and p. 282.

13. *Ibid.*, p. 270.

Chapter Three

1. *Pied Piper of Lovers* (London, 1935). This edition is listed in: Robert Potter and Brooke Whiting, *Lawrence Durrell: A Checklist* (Los Angeles, 1961), p. 8. But neither the facilities of the British Museum nor the network of American libraries is able to produce or reproduce a copy at this time. The Potter and Whiting *Checklist* includes 311 items—through 1961. The Durrell canon is long, detailed, and complicated. The *Checklist* here cited will be referred to in this study as "Potter and Whiting."

2. *A Private Correspondence,* p. 60.

3. *Ibid.,* p. 3

4. It's Durrell's first *available* novel. References in this study are to the American edition: *Panic Spring,* by Charles Norden (New York, 1937), but see Potter and Whiting, items 13 and 14. Copies of this American edition are fairly well distributed among the American university libraries.

5. A few years ago, referring to his early writing, Durrell said: "All the work I did before I heard the sound of my own voice is hardly worth investigation." Kenneth Young, "Dialogue with Durrell," *Encounter,* XIII (December, 1959), p. 67.

6. *The Black Book* has a complicated publishing history. Portions of it appeared in 1937 in *The Booster.* The first edition was published by Kahane (Paris) in 1938. (See: Potter and Whiting, items 10, 19, 30, 223, 224, 251 for the various subsequent editions.)

7. References in this study are to the American edition (New York, 1960) which is identical in pagination with the Dutton Paperback, D 115 (1963).

8. P. 109. A "negus" is a beverage made of hot water, wine, and lemon juice, named after Col. Negus, who died in 1732.

9. (October, 1960) p. 120.

10. See: Potter and Whiting, items 97, 205 for early editions. The edition referred to here is the first American edition: *The Dark Labyrinth* (New York, 1962). In general this new-old book was reviewed in America with controlled enthusiasm for recognizable aspects and traits of the Alexandrian Durrell.

11. *A Private Correspondence,* p. 201.

12. See items 198, 199, and 303. The edition referred to here is the American edition (New York, 1957).

13. *Times Literary Supplement* (May 31, 1957), p. xviii.

Chapter Four

1. See note 4 to Chapter Two above for editions used in this study.

2. References to Toby Mannering occur in Clea's and Darley's imitations of Scobie's monologues (C:85ff). Toby is memorable for his many schemes, such as a plan to sell parts of the Pharos as paperweights (C:243). "Budgie" is the famous maker of "earth-closets" (C:261ff) to whom Scobie was writing just before he died (B:140). His full name is Charles Donahue Budgeon. Abdul appears first as an unscrupulous barber (B:35ff), and later as the half-blind caretaker of the shrine of "El Scob" (C:80ff).

3. The theory of the "space-time novel" makes possible an infinite

number of projections of the characters and events beyond the arbitrarily limited pages of the book. See Chapter Five below.

4. Clea later tells Darley of Fosca's cremation and the scattering of her ashes in the desert by Pombal. A note in the first volume appended to a reference to Fosca by Arnauti (*J*:76) gives a quite different version of her death: "Fosca died in childbirth . . ." (*J*:253). This "note" and the meaningless reference to a "green fingerstall" (*J*:245) is omitted in the one volume edition (New York, 1962).

5. An index to *all* the characters in the *Quartet* would contain over one hundred names. In *Balthazar* there are two long lists of names of Alexandrians (*B*:45, 218), but many of those listed remain merely names. Others, however, emerge as substantial characters as the story progresses. Space limitations do not allow a complete index here, but as a convenience to students of the *Quartet*, names and identifications for twenty-two characters not included in the summaries in this chapter are listed below:

ALI: Narouz' factor with "cropped ears" (*B*:69). Referred to in Nessim's diary as a Negro eunuch (*M*:32), Ali is present at "Karm" just before Narouz is murdered, then disappears (*M*:302ff). Later Ali appears as the last servant at "Karm" (*C*:50). Also a boatman who helps Pombal when Fosca is killed—probably not the same person (*C*:211).

AMAR: Toto's homosexual lover, accused of Toto's murder, then acquitted (*B*:212ff).

ATHENA TRASHE: A friend of the Cervonis, at whose carnival ball she makes love to Jacques on a pile of dominoes containing Toto's dead body (*B*:211ff). Narouz likes her because she uses the same perfume as Leila (*B*:195). She appears at Semira's debut, which she helps direct, wearing "silver crickets in her ears" (*C*:91).

BALBZ: Balthazar's dentist, who apparently discovers Toto's dead body at the Cervonis' ball (*B*:195ff). He is later referred to as that "droning Pierre Balbz, who drank opium because it made the 'bones blossom'" (*C*:91).

CERVONI: identified as "General," a stately Alexandrian who entertains other Alexandrians. The "Cervonis" appear at Justine's wedding (*B*:99), give the carnival ball at which Toto is murdered (*B*:192ff), and help with Balthazar's rehabilitation (*C*:72ff).

DONKIN: Mountolive's "third secretary," youthful, bearded, who "smokes like a girl" but is not without intelligence and sensibilities (*M*:237ff). He and his wife are described by Pursewarden as "the only nice ones" (*M*:102).

Errol: Head of Chancery in Cairo. He plays the competent-subordinate role to Mountolive. He is suspicious of Pursewarden from the start (*M*:90ff). In general he proves to be "right" throughout Mountolive's critical early days as Ambassador (*M*:133ff). He and his wife Angela are described by Pursewarden as "formidably Britannic" (*M*:102). It is Angela who presents Mountolive with the "sausage dog" named Fluke (*M*:298).

Father Paul: Roman Catholic Chaplain, Nessim's friend, who is "folded into his religion like a razor into its case" (*J*:159). He appears at Scobie's funeral (*B*:174), and also at Fosca's funeral, where he is described as "porcine" (*C*:215ff).

Father Racine: A botanist, Darley's colleague at the school in upper Egypt. He is described as the "most sensitive and intelligent of them all" (*J*:234).

Granier: Intelligence official to whom Mountolive reports at the Foreign Office in London before going to Egypt as Ambassador. Although seen only once, Granier is sympathetically characterized as "one of those worldly Catholics who regard God as a congenial club-member whose motives are above question" (*M*:87ff).

Grishkin: Russian ballet dancer who becomes the young Mountolive's mistress after he has left Alexandria (and Leila). She is apparently pregnant by Mountolive when he leaves her (*M*:53ff).

Hamid: The one-eyed Berber servant who "looks after" the apartment where Darley and Pombal live in *Justine*. Hamid had been half-blinded when a lad by his mother—to avoid conscription. Said to be "djinn-ridden" (*J*:87), he is a pious Mohammedan given to many kinds of superstition. Inscrutable, a listener at doors, Hamid appears at certain critical moments as the bearer of tidings, the liaison man between lovers, and the sympathetic and ever-faithful servant. In *Clea* he lives in the little box-room once occupied by Melissa, to whose memory he remains devoted. He is, to Darley, a link with the past.

Kenilworth: Jealous contemporary of Mountolive, head of Personnel, London Foreign Office. He warns Mountolive against Pursewarden (*M*:86ff). Darley describes him as "fat" but "not unamiable" (*C*:34ff). He once dropped in on James Joyce. (*C*:137).

Nimrod: A vaguely outlined character. According to Balthazar, Nimrod is homosexual. As an official of the Secretariat, he investigates Scobie's and Toto's deaths (*B*:172ff, 215ff). Later he investigates Pursewarden's suicide (*M*:180). He also tells the story of Budgie's earth-closets (*C*:261ff).

Nur: An Egyptian official involved in the prosecution of the case against Nessim. Nur is described as "timid and ape-like" (*M*:250). His ineffectiveness as an official delays the action against Nessim.

PORDRE: French Consul-General. Pombal's "Chief" is described as "a whim rather than a man" (*J*:171). He and Pombal join the Free French in Egypt during the war.

RAFAEL: Barber, procurer, friend of Memlik (*M*:257). A corrupt Alexandrian, Rafael advises Memlik to exploit Narouz as the victim rather than Nessim.

RANDIDI: An Alexandrian referred to at first by Nessim in passing (*B*:94). Later Balthazar says Randidi's daughter took poison and Randidi hanged himself—all as a result of Balthazar's hoax-story of an invented lover (*M*:234-35).

SELIM: Nessim's laconic and impassive secretary-servant. Selim is seen most frequently in *Justine* where he goes about Nessim's business. For example, he calls upon Melissa after she has warned Nessim of his wife's unfaithfulness (*J*:199). It is possible that he has been suborned by Maskelyne, but in general he is inscrutable and apparently faithful.

TAOR: The woman saint whom Narouz visits (*M*:126). Taor exerts a significant influence on Narouz, as Nessim realizes (*M*:225ff). Melissa's daughter's "body-servant and *amah*" is also called Taor (*C*:196).

TELFORD: British War Office official in Egypt, second in command to Maskelyne, whom he worships. Telford is first described by Pursewarden as "a large blotchy ingratiating civilian with ill-fitting dentures . . ." (*M*:107). He is one of the many righteous minor officials satirized in the *Quartet*. Telford's "discomfort" at irregular events, such as Pursewarden's suicide, is usually exorcised in a typed report. Characteristically enough, his wife (Mavis) is a "fattish little duck . . ." (*C*:157).

ZOLTAN: The proprietor of the café where Melissa worked (*B*:210). Zoltan appears later at the *Auberge Bleue* as "resplendent *maître d'hôtel*" (*C*:91). Interestingly, two of his brief appearances in the *Quartet* are associated with mackintoshes: one Pursewarden's (*M*:166) and one Darley's (*C*:40).

Chapter Five

1. *Clea*, pp. 135-36. Pursewarden is advising Darley. See note 4 to Chapter Two above for editions used in this study.

2. Many of my ideas concerning narrators and their "reliability" have been stimulated by Wayne Booth's careful analysis of certain aspects of fiction: *The Rhetoric of Fiction* (Chicago, 1961).

3. See "Author's Note" which prefaces *Clea*.

4. "I began to see too that the real 'fiction' lay neither in Arnauti's pages nor Pursewarden's—nor even my own. It was life itself that was a fiction—we were all saying it in our different ways, each understanding it according to his nature and gift." *Clea*, p. 177.

Chapter Six

1. Durrell's "Note," which introduces *Balthazar* and which includes this statement, is perhaps ironic. In it he denies that his work is "Proustian or Joycean method," and he sets himself apart from Bergson's famous "duration." Scholars and philosophers may waste much time studying and arguing the fine points of Bergsonism, Wyndham Lewisism, and Durrellism—if Durrell is only having fun!

2. It is not easy to trace the sources of love and lovers. Sex and its cousin, love (and perhaps pornography), are constantly repristinating themselves to meet new needs, yet their techniques are as old as the hills.

3. This "fun," of course, is high-level and magnificently intricate sport.

4. The delightful depravities of de Sade's *Justine* may have influenced Durrell's *Justine*. Durrell read de Sade—and so probably did *his* Justine.

5. Awareness of the sea in the *Quartet* is ubiquitous. When Clea asks Scobie if he misses the sea, he replies: "Every night I put to sea in my dreams" (*J*:251). Darley, on his island, works upon the "raw material" of the story in "long and passionate self-communings over a winter sea" (*B*:135). And the final memorable summer, prelude to the resolution in *Clea*, brings about a "curious sea-engendered *rapport*" between Clea and Darley: "A delight almost as deep as the bondage of kisses—to enter the rhythm of the waters together, responding to each other and the play of the long tides" (*C*:228).

6. *Balthazar*, p. 142. Pursewarden uses "will" instead of "shall" and "care" instead of "cares"—not serious errors.

7. For example, Kenneth Rexroth (see "Selected Bibliography" below) cooled off after his initial enthusiasms. Other reviewers also became bolder as they increasingly suspected that Durrell was "serious" about his story.

Chapter Seven

1. For the various editions of *Esprit de Corps* and *Stiff Upper Lip* see: Potter and Whiting, items 185, 208, 217, 244, 288, 301. The edition referred to here is the one most easily available to American readers. The two works are bound together as one volume but are paged separately: *Esprit de Corps and Stiff Upper Lip* (New York, 1961).

Notes and References

This Dutton paperback edition includes two sketches, "La Valise" and "Cry Wolf," not included in the 1957 Faber edition of *Esprit,* and one sketch "A Smircher Smirched," not included in the 1958 Faber edition of *Stiff Upper Lip.* Other "Antrobus" sketches have appeared elsewhere, but this doubleheader volume is a more than adequate sampling of Durrell's "Wodehouse manner." Durrell's humor, good-natured and healthy as it is, tends to repeat itself.

2. Early in 1958 Durrell wrote to Miller: "I didn't send you *Esprit de Corps;* thought you mightn't find it funny. I had to pay for the baby's shoes somehow and wrote it in a very short time. To my surprise *Harper's, Atlantic,* etc. bought bits, so perhaps it is not too British after all—or perhaps Americans sometimes enjoy sodden British jokes. . . . They take me twenty minutes to write. Only 1000 words. All this is very perplexing to my fans who don't know whether I am P. G. Wodehouse or James Joyce or what the hell." *A Private Correspondence,* pp. 327-28.

Chapter Eight

1. Although there are more articles classifiable as travel writing than are here reviewed, the restriction of the discussion in this study to three books and one series of articles seems defensible. In 1959 Durrell told the *Paris Review* interviewers: "I've done hundreds and thousands of words of feature articles, all buried in remote periodicals. Some under my own name, some under initials. . . ." *Writers at Work* (Second Series), p. 268. No one has yet been tempted to dig up all those words.

2. For editions of *Prospero's Cell, Reflections on a Marine Venus,* and *Bitter Lemons* see: Potter and Whiting: items 82, 157, 182, 203, 221, 222, 274, and 276. References here are to *Prospero's Cell and Reflections on a Marine Venus.* (Dutton Paperback: D 95, 1962) and *Bitter Lemons,* (Dutton Paperback: D 44, 1959).

3. Durrell "engineered" the move for his whole family. See Gerald Durrell, *My Family and Other Animals* (New York, 1957).

4. Freya Stark, *New York Times Book Review* (November 6, 1960), p. 7.

5. Articles reviewed in this study include the following:

"The Worldly University of Grenoble," *Holiday,* XXV (January, 1959), pp. 48-51+.

"Ripe Living in Provence," *Holiday* XXVI (November, 1959), pp. 70-75+.

"The Rhone," *Holiday,* XXVII (January, 1960), pp. 68-73+.

"Geneva," *Holiday,* XXIX (January, 1961), pp. 54-55+.

"Laura: A Portrait of Avignon," *Holiday*, XXIX (February, 1961), pp. 58-63+.

"In Praise of Fanatics," *Holiday*, XXXII (August, 1962), pp. 66-70+.

"The Gascon Touch," *Holiday*, XXXIII (January, 1963), pp. 68-74+.

Chapter Nine

1. Inevitably plays are classified as Cornelian ("a drama of the will versus emotion") or Racinian ("the conflict of two emotions"). The definitions are from Lander MacClintock, who identifies *Acte* as the former, *Sappho* as the latter. See: "Durrell's Plays," in *The World of Lawrence Durrell*, ed. by Harry T. Moore (Carbondale, Illinois: 1962), pp. 66-86.

2. For the publishing history of *Sappho* see: Potter and Whiting, items 131, 141, 216, 243. The edition referred to here (identical with the 1950 British edition and the 1958 American reissue of the 1950 British Faber edition) is as follows: *Sappho: A Play in Verse* (London, 1960).

According to Durrell there are four versions of *Acte*—none of which he "really" likes (personal correspondence). I have seen two texts, one in English and one in German, but my discussion is based upon the German text used in the Hamburg performance rather than upon the longer English text, for Durrell wrote this play for the theater and the revisions called for by production and agreed to by the author are incorporated in the text translated from Durrell's version into German by Robert Schnorr. In this version, for example, a "dwarf jester," is omitted entirely, as well as several expository (and relatively dull) scenes. See "Actis: Drama in drei Akten von Lawrence Durrell," *Theater Heute* (January, 1962), pp. iii-xx. The version most convenient for American readers is printed in *Show*, I (December, 1961), pp. 45-55, 95-105. "An Author's Note" included there gives a clear statement of Durrell's intentions (and hopes) regarding the play.

An Irish Faustus has been published both in America and England. The text referred to here is as follows: *An Irish Faustus* (New York, 1964).

3. *A Private Correspondence,* p. 285 and p. 282.

4. See note 2 above. Durrell has asked that this work be considered in a "provisional light" (personal correspondence). The director-producer of the Hamburg performances of *Actis* was the late, great Gustaf Gründgens—whose advice and friendship certainly deeply influenced Durrell. For a characteristic review of the Hamburg perform-

ance of *Actis* (as it was called there) see "Durrell and Co." [by Sarah Gainham], *Spectator,* CCVIII (January 19, 1962), p. 61.

5. "The critics were divided. Willy Haas of *Die Welt* said it was 'astonishing what Durrell made out of this trite subject.' Werner Thamms of the *West-deutsche Allgemeine* said 'I'm not completely satisfied. It's neither fish nor fowl.'" *New York Times* (November 23, 1961), 50:2.

6. Durrell apparently contributed to the script of the film, *Cleopatra,* and has sold the movie rights of the *Quartet* as well as of an unpublished novella called "Judith." See *New York Times* (December 1, 1963), X5:6.

Chapter Ten

1. In "An Author's Note" prefacing his second verse play Durrell wrote: "I think it is to T. S. Eliot we owe the phrase 'heightened speech'; it is something for which he hunted long and patiently. . . . I am conducting the same sort of hunt for myself. . . ." See *Show,* I (December, 1961), p. 47.

2. *Ibid.,* p. 101.

3. Curtis Cate, "Lawrence Durrell," *Atlantic Monthly,* 208:6 (December, 1961), p. 69.

4. Peter Dickinson, "A Clutch of Poets," *Punch,* CCXXXVIII (1960), p. 740.

5. B.G.D. [rev. of *Collected Poems*], *Books Abroad,* 35 (1961), p. 138.

6. R. W. Flint, "A Major Novelist," *Commentary,* XXVII: 4 (April, 1959), pp. 353-56.

7. "One Vote for the Sun," *The World of Lawrence Durrell,* ed. Harry T. Moore (Carbondale, Illinois, 1962), p. 150.

8. "A Minority Report," *Ibid.,* p. 140.

9. Benjamin De Mott, "Grading the Emanglons," *Hudson Review,* XIII: 3 (1960), p. 464.

10. Julian Mitchell and Gene Andrewski, "Lawrence Durrell," *Writers at Work: The Paris Review Interviews, Second Series,* (New York, 1963), p. 282.

Selected Bibliography

PRIMARY SOURCES

The selected bibliography of Durrell's works is limited to items conveniently available to American readers. All individually published poems, notes, sketches, and articles, all items published in periodicals except *Acte*, all prefaces, all items merely edited, and all translations except *Pope Joan* have been omitted. There are 311 items attributed to Durrell through 1961 in the most comprehensive checklist now available: Potter, Robert and Brooke Whiting. *Lawrence Durrell: A Checklist*. Los Angeles: 1961.

"Acte," *Show*, I (December, 1961), 45-55, 95-105.
The Alexandria Quartet (one volume edition). New York: E. P. Dutton, 1962.
Art and Outrage: A Correspondence about Henry Miller between Lawrence Durrell and Alfred Perlès, with Intermissions by Henry Miller. New York: E. P. Dutton, 1961.
Balthazar. New York: E. P. Dutton, 1958. Dutton Paperback, 1961.
Bitter Lemons. New York: E. P. Dutton, 1958. Dutton Paperback, 1959.
The Black Book. New York: E. P. Dutton, 1960. Dutton Paperback, 1963.
Clea. New York: E. P. Dutton, 1960. Dutton Paperback, 1961.
Collected Poems. New York: E. P. Dutton, 1960.
The Dark Labyrinth. New York: E. P. Dutton, 1962. Dutton Paperback, 1964. (Originally published as *Cefalû*. London: Editions Poetry, 1947.)
Esprit de Corps. New York: E. P. Dutton, 1958. Issued together with *Stiff Upper Lip*. Dutton Paperback, 1961.
An Irish Faustus. New York: E. P. Dutton, 1964.
Justine. New York: E. P. Dutton, 1957. Dutton Paperback, 1961.
A Key to Modern British Poetry. Norman, Oklahoma: University of Oklahoma Press, 1952.

Lawrence Durrell and Henry Miller: A Private Correspondence. Edited by George Wickes. New York: E. P. Dutton, 1963. Dutton Paperback, 1965.

Mountolive. New York: E. P. Dutton, 1959. Dutton Paperback, 1961.

Panic Spring. By Charles Norden [pseudonym]. New York: Covici-Friede, 1937.

The Poetry of Lawrence Durrell. New York: Dutton Paperback, 1962.

Pope Joan, by Emmanuel Royidis. Translated from the Greek by Lawrence Durrell. New York: E. P. Dutton, 1961.

Prospero's Cell. New York: E. P. Dutton, 1960. Issued together with *Reflections on a Marine Venus.* Dutton Paperback, 1962.

Reflections on a Marine Venus. New York: E. P. Dutton, 1960. Issued together with *Prospero's Cell.* Dutton Paperback, 1962.

Sappho: A Play in Verse. London: Faber and Faber, 1960.

Selected Poems. New York: Grove Press, 1956.

Stiff Upper Lip. New York: E. P. Dutton, 1959. Issued together with *Esprit de Corps.* Dutton Paperback, 1961.

White Eagles Over Serbia. New York: Criterion Books, 1957.

2. Recordings by Lawrence Durrell

Grecian Echoes. Lausanne, Switzerland: LVA 1003-4. Selections from *Bitter Lemons, Prospero's Cell,* and *Reflections on a Marine Venus,* effectively chosen and charmingly read by Durrell.

An Irish Faust. Lausanne, Switzerland: LVA 201. A coherent and evocative reading of most of the verse play published as *An Irish Faustus.*

The Love Poems of Lawrence Durrell. New Rochelle, New York: Spoken Arts, Inc. A generous selection of poems read with finesse by the poet himself—recorded in Montpellier, France. The record jacket contains a delightful account of the congenial recording session.

3. Important Interviews with Lawrence Durrell

"Lawrence Durrell Answers a Few Questions," *Two Cities* (Paris), April 15, 1959, 25-28. Also in: Moore, Harry T. ed. *The World of Lawrence Durrell.* Carbondale: Southern Illinois University Press, 1962. Durrell refers in this brief but pointed interview to his "characters" as "my pets, my toys, my inventions, my recreation, my only way of earning my living."

"Lawrence Durrell Vous Parle," *Réalités* (Paris), No. 178 (November, 1960), 105ff. The novelist responds courteously, wittily, and honestly to the usual questions, and ends by noting emphatically the importance of "solitude"—and by implication, the threat posed by interviewers.

Mitchell, Julian, and Gene Andrewski. "The Art of Fiction XXXIII: Lawrence Durrell," *The Paris Review*, No. 22 (Autumn-Winter, 1959-60), 33-61. Also in: *Writers at Work: The Paris Review Interviews (Second Series)*. New York: Viking, 1963, 257-82. Durrell is interviewed at his home in the Midi, and explains his exile as necessary to his welfare as an artist. He courteously probes his work and psyche for the persistent questioners.

Young, Kenneth. "A Dialogue with Durrell," *Encounter*, XIII (December, 1959), 61-68. Shortly after this lively interview, in which Durrell discusses his life, works, and ideas, the novelist cautioned the interviewer: "Next year I might believe the opposite of all I believe today!"

SECONDARY SOURCES

1. *Articles and Books about Durrell*

ARBAN, DOMINIQUE. "Lawrence Durrell," *Preuves*, 109 (1960), 86-94. A typically enthusiastic and continental endorsement of Durrell's greatness by a professional critic and lecturer.

ARTHOS, JOHN. "Lawrence Durrell's Gnosticism," *The Personalist*, XLIII (1961), 360-73. A serious and thoughtfully considered charge is levelled against Durrell's philosophical and artistic positions, which do not "square" with one another.

BALDANZA, FRANK. "Lawrence Durrell's Word Continuum," *Critique*, IV: 2 (Spring-Summer, 1961), 3-17. After a careful explication of Durrell's "theory" and its sources, the effectiveness of the *Quartet* is measured in this thoughtful essay.

CATE, CURTIS. "Lawrence Durrell," *Atlantic Monthly*, 208:6 (December, 1961), 63-69. The freshest parts of this literate essay begin: "Durrell remarked to me one day as we sat at a sidewalk café in Nimes . . ."

CORKE, HILARY. "Mr. Durrell and Brother Criticus," *Encounter*, XIV (May, 1960), 65ff. This amusing review article indicts critics who downgrade Durrell. Durrell is defended as master of his craft and competent in his subject areas, such as Alexandria and love.

DEMOTT, BENJAMIN. "Grading the Emanglons," *Hudson Review*,

XIII: 3 (Autumn, 1960), 457-64. The critic enjoys himself in this immoderate attack on Durrell's "Gothic gimcracks," manipulated structure, and second-rate ideas in the *Quartet.*

DENNIS, NIGEL. "New Four-Star King of Novelists," *Life,* 49 (November 21, 1960), 96-109. A somewhat sensational sketch of Durrell by a British novelist for a spectacular American periodical.

DURRELL, GERALD. *My Family and Other Animals.* New York: Viking, 1957. Brother Gerald, a naturalist, writes warmly of life on Corfu —and of "Larry."

ESKIN, STANLEY G. "Durrell's Themes in *The Alexandria Quartet,*" *Texas Quarterly,* (Winter, 1962), 43-60. The "themes," which are spelled out, add up to a "genuine Durrellian vision of the world."

FLINT, R. W. "A Major Novelist," *Commentary,* XXVII: 4 (April, 1959), 353-56. This reviewer realizes that "Durrell has set a trap for reviewers" and so juggles the variables nicely and comes out a Durrell-enthusiast.

GÉRARD, ALBERT. "Lawrence Durrell: Un Grand Talent de Basse Epoque," *Révue Générale Belge* (Oct., 1962), 15-29. A thoughtful thesis carefully supported: The defects of the *Quartet* make it "ominously appropriate" to our purposeless age.

GORDON, AMBROSE. "Time, Space, and Eros: *The Alexandria Quartet* Rehearsed," in *Six Contemporary Novels.* Austin, Texas: University of Texas Press, 1962. Durrell is in good company in this volume. The other five novelists are Pasternak, C. P. Snow, Hemingway, Faulkner, and Beckett.

HAGAPIAN, JOHN V. "The Resolution of *The Alexandria Quartet,*" *Critique,* VII (1964), 97-106. Theme and form are unified at the end of the *Quartet* through a kind of "conjunction of love and time."

HIGHET, GILBERT. "The Alexandrians of Lawrence Durrell," *Horizon,* II (March, 1960), 113-18. The *Quartet* is seen as a serious work in which Proustian and exotic elements combine with relativity theory to search out "truth."

HUTCHENS, ELEANOR N. "The Heraldic Universe in *The Alexandria Quartet,*" *College English,* 24:1 (October, 1962), 56-61. An important and intimate relationship between the *Quartet* and *The Waste Land* is here demonstrated.

LEVIDOVA, I. "A Four-Decker in Stagnant Waters," *Anglo-Soviet Journal,* (Summer, 1962), 39-41. This critic, annoyed at praise of Durrell in the "bourgeois press" describes the *Quartet* as a "vividly painted" ship unable to set sail.

Selected Bibliography

LITTLEJOHN, DAVID. "Lawrence Durrell: The Novelist as Entertainer," *Motive*, 23 (November, 1962), 14-16. The *Quartet* is seen as "refreshing"—against the sordidness of contemporary novelists like Bellow, Malamud, and Updike.

LUND, MARY GRAHAM. "The Alexandrian Projection," *Antioch Review*, XXX:1 (Summer, 1961), 193ff. Sound explication combines with praise and devotion to exalt the *Quartet*. Durrell is put in the grand tradition along with such giants as Homer, Dante, Rabelais, Shakespeare, Goethe, Blake, and Dostoyevsky.

————. "Durrell: Soft Focus on Crime," Prairie Schooner, XXXV (1961), 339-44. In Durrell's world "things are grotesque reflections of deep psychological realities."

————. "Submerge for Reality: The New Novel Form of Lawrence Durrell," *Southwest Review*, XLIV (Summer, 1959), 229-35. Durrell is enthusiastically defended as neither decadent nor overly symbolic.

MOORE, HARRY T., ed. *The World of Lawrence Durrell*. Carbondale: Southern Illinois University Press, 1962. Also New York: Dutton Paperback, 1964. This collection of articles and other items relating to Durrell is distinguished. It forms a convenient survey of the best that has been written about Durrell, pro and con, through 1961. Items included in this collection are not repeated in the bibliography here. The collection includes essays by Richard Aldington, Carl Bode, Victor Brombert, Bonamy Dobrée, Hayden Carruth, George P. Elliott, Martin Green, Lander Mac-Clintock, Cecily Mackworth, Henry Miller, Harry T. Moore, Derek Stanford, George Steiner, Gerald Sykes, Lionel Trilling. There are also letters to Durrell from G. D. Wotton and W.D.G. Cox, two interviews with Durrell, and several letters from Durrell to Jean Fanchette not published elsewhere.

MORGAN, THOMAS B. "The Autumnal Arrival of Lawrence Durrell," *Esquire*, (September, 1960), 108-11. This informal and anecdotal recreation includes some usual and some not quite so usual comments by Durrell himself.

O'BRIEN, R. A. "Time, Space, and Language in Lawrence Durrell," *Waterloo Review*, 6 (Winter, 1961), 16-24. Durrell is related to Proust, Woolf, Joyce, Faulkner, and Anthony Powell in the distinction he makes between clock-time and psychological time. Durrell here is rated as much superior to Salinger and Hemingway.

PERLÈS, ALFRED. *My Friend Lawrence Durrell*. Northwood, Middlesex: Scorpion Press, 1961. This intense account of certain aspects of Durrell's life and works gets its special validity from the personal friendship between Durrell and Perlès.

PROSER, MATTHEW N. "Darley's Dilemma: The Problem of Structure in Durrell's *Alexandria Quartet,*" *Critique,* IV: 2 (Spring-Summer, 1961), 18-28. The *Quartet* is "better than ordinary melodrama"—but just how much better seems debatable: the work, however, is "provocative and in many ways a resplendent *tour de force.*"

REXROTH, KENNETH. "Lawrence Durrell," in *Assays.* New York: New Directions Paperback, 1962, 118-30. Between 1957 and 1960 Rexroth changed from "devoted fan" to sharp critic, finding *Clea* much inferior to earlier volumes.

THOMAS, ALAN G., and LAWRENCE G. POWELL. "Some Uncollected Authors XXIII: Lawrence Durrell," *Book Collector,* IX (Spring, 1960), 56-63. Durrell, like Kipling, has produced many "scarce and fragile items" eagerly sought after by collectors. Thomas, a personal friend of Durrell, reminisces pleasantly and admiringly.

UNTERECKER, JOHN. *Lawrence Durrell.* New York and London: Columbia University Press, 1964. This insightful, pamphlet-length study of Durrell emphasizes the writer's "infinite variety" *and* his "marble constancy." The analysis of the *Quartet* is especially perceptive.

WEATHERHEAD, A. K. "Romantic Anachronism in *The Alexandria Quartet,*" *Modern Fiction Studies,* 10:2 (Summer, 1964), 128-36. The *Quartet* differs from the main stream of novels in its emphasis on free will. Durrell's work shows the influence of Groddeck, the psychologist who believed man *chose* to be well or ill.

2. Background and Reference Works

ALLEN, WALTER. *The Modern Novel in Britain and the United States.* New York: Dutton, 1964. This excellent discussion of the *really* modern novel (1920-1960) places Durrell in the Joyce-Proust tradition, but Durrell suffers by comparison with the two giants.

BERGSON, HENRI. *Time and Free Will.* New York: Harper Torchbook, 1960. This reprint is a good source of original Bergsonism as contrasted with the derived and distorted ideas in Wyndham Lewis and others. Durrell probably knew this work before writing the *Quartet.*

BOOTH, WAYNE C. *The Rhetoric of Fiction.* Chicago: University of Chicago Press, 1961. Booth's careful study, one of the first to wrestle with the subject, is the most helpful in its analysis of reliable and unreliable narrators in fiction.

CAVAFY, C. P. *The Complete Poems of Cavafy*, Trans. by Rae Dalven. New York: Harcourt, Brace and World, 1961. The erotic Alexandrian poet, whose style, charm, and dignity obviously impressed Durrell, is here nicely presented in readable translation.

FORSTER, E. M. *Alexandria: A History and a Guide*. New York: Anchor Books, 1961. As good as a trip to Alexandria: this is a useful travel guide to the *physical* aspects of Durrell's otherwise fantasied city.

————. *Pharos and Pharillon*. New York: Knopf, 1962. The mood and spirit of ancient and modern Alexandria is projected in these literate essays.

GINDIN, JAMES. *Postwar British Fiction: New Accents and Attitudes*. Berkeley, California: University of California Press, 1962. Durrell is included here in the section entitled "Some Current Fads." The critic's hostility is both specific and general. His bias calls Angus Wilson the "best"—and C. P. Snow, Colin Wilson, and Durrell the "most overrated."

KARL, FREDERICK R. *The Contemporary English Novel*. New York: Farrar, Straus and Cudahy, 1962. This general and particular discussion of Durrell and his contemporaries needs to be read critically.

KERMODE, FRANK. *Puzzles and Epiphanies*. New York: Chilmark Press, 1962. This collection of "essays and reviews" (1958-1961) by a professional critic provides orientation for the student of post-war fiction. Of Durrell, Kermode says: "I have blown hot and cold over his work . . ." (p. 227).

KUMAR, SHIV K. *Bergson and the Stream of Consciousness Novel*. New York: New York University Press, 1963. "Bergsonism" is both negatively and positively related to Durrell's experiment in spacetime. This discussion is an adequate introduction to the concept.

LEWIS, WYNDHAM. *Time and Western Man*. Boston: Beacon Press, 1957. Durrell's Pursewarden sometimes resembles Lewis. This philosophical work is pretentious and controversial. Lewis thought *he* understood space and time better than both Joyce and Proust.

MENDILOW, A. A. *Time and the Novel*. London: Peter Nevil, 1952. The modern obsession with "time" explains the form and technique of the novel. Bergsonian "duration" is of the essence.

MEYERHOFF, HANS. *Time in Literature*. Berkeley, California: University of California Press, 1960. References to Joyce, Proust, and others are provocative and contribute to the sophistication needed to apprehend Durrell's "space-time."

MILLER, HENRY. *Tropic of Cancer*. New York: Grove Press, 1961. This is the book that ignited Durrell.

——. *The Colossus of Maroussi*. New York: New Directions Paperback, n.d. Miller's "incandescent" account of Corfu and Greece includes many references to Durrell.

SUZUKI, DAISETZ T. *The Essentials of Zen Buddhism,* ed. Bernard Phillips. New York: E. P. Dutton, 1962. Miller and Durrell studied "Suzuki."

WAITE, AUTHUR EDWARD. *The Pictorial Key to the Tarot*. New Hyde Park: University Books, 1959. An esoteric explanation of the mysteries of the cards which Durrell and T. S. Eliot certainly knew.

Index